Core Knowledge Preschool Sequence

Content & Skill Guidelines for Preschool

Core Knowledge Foundation

Acknowledgments

The Core Knowledge Foundation would like to thank the many, many dedicated education professionals whose interests and efforts are reflected in this document. We would particularly like to thank the many French preschool teachers who enthusiastically welcomed us into their diverse classes, as well as the many preschool teachers at Core Knowledge and other schools who have been committed to this project and have provided much helpful feedback. Special recognition is due Catherine Howanstine, St. Leonard's Elementary School, Calvert County, Maryland, and Debbie Riley, Three Oaks Elementary School, Ft. Myers, Florida, who so generously gave of their time and expertise.

ART DIRECTION AND DESIGN: Bill Womack Incorporated

Contents

The Core Knowledge Preschool Sequence

THE CORE KNOWLEDGE PRESCHOOL SEQUENCE: WHAT IS IT?

The Core Knowledge Preschool Sequence is a set of model guidelines describing fundamental competencies and specific knowledge that, for children from three to five years of age, can provide a solid, coherent foundation for later learning in kindergarten and beyond.

EXCELLENCE AND FAIRNESS

The Preschool Sequence is offered as another practical step toward the Core Knowledge Foundation's goal of promoting greater excellence and fairness in early education. Internationally, the most successful educational systems teach a core of knowledge in the early grades. Only by explicitly specifying the competencies and knowledge that all children should share can we guarantee equal access to those competencies and knowledge. In our current system, disadvantaged children especially suffer from low expectations that often translate into "waiting until they are ready" and watered-down curricula.

When expectations are made explicit, however, disadvantaged children, like all children, are exposed to a coherent core of challenging, interesting competencies and knowledge. This background not only provides a foundation for later learning, but also makes up the common ground for communication in a diverse society.

INTENDED USE OF THE PRESCHOOL SEQUENCE

The Preschool Sequence is intended to guide the planning of experiences and activities for preschool children by offering a coherent progression of skills and knowledge in the following areas:

PHYSICAL WELL-BEING AND MOTOR DEVELOPMENT
- Movement and Coordination

SOCIAL AND EMOTIONAL DEVELOPMENT
- Autonomy & Social Skills

APPROACHES TO LEARNING
- Work Habits

LANGUAGE
- Oral Language
- Nursery Rhymes, Poems, Fingerplays and Songs
- Storybook Reading and Storytelling
- Emerging Literacy Skills in Reading and Writing

KNOWLEDGE ACQUISITION AND COGNITIVE DEVELOPMENT
- Mathematical Reasoning and Number Sense
- Orientation in Time and Space
- Scientific Reasoning and the Physical World
- Music
- Visual Arts

"LANGUAGE OF INSTRUCTION" IN THE PRESCHOOL SEQUENCE

It is almost impossible to overemphasize the significance of early language development and its impact upon nearly all other aspects of development. For this reason, the Preschool Sequence addresses language skills not only in the "Language" section but throughout the Sequence.

Research in language development reveals that children need to hear language, specific words or vocabulary, grammatical features, and so on, before making it their own. When children hear certain words or phrases used repeatedly, they first acquire an understanding of the word or phrase; with repeated exposure in different situations, they will eventually begin using those same words and phrases in their own speech. Thus it is especially important that preschool children hear the language and vocabulary typically used in school to talk about specific subjects and content. For this reason, the Preschool Sequence includes in each discipline a subsection called "Language of Instruction," which lists terms that knowledgeable and competent individuals generally use to talk about the particular subject. While not comprehensive or exhaustive, the lists provide a starting point, a suggested sampling of the precise vocabulary to which young children should be exposed.

It is important to stress that the word lists are not intended for use in isolated drill or memorization. These are not terms that the children are expected to memorize or necessarily use at this time in their own speech. At this stage, the aim for young children is exposure, that is, laying the foundation for understanding such language when it is used by others. As noted earlier, children need to hear a word used repeatedly in different situations before making it their own.

The lists are included to serve as a guide for teachers and caregivers as they interact and talk with children during the course of various activities. Such vocabulary may be incorporated in adult comments that describe what the child is doing (or, what the adult is doing, especially if he or she is modeling a behavior or approach). By using language in this way, adults demonstrate that experience can be represented symbolically by language. Furthermore, restatements in the form of questions, using the same precise vocabulary, will invite children to listen actively and begin to assimilate the language being used. More specific examples illustrating how to use the language of instruction terms in this way are included with each list. Also, see the "Language of Instruction" in the Implementation section.

SPECIFICITY AND READINESS

The Core Knowledge Preschool Sequence is distinguished by its specificity. It identifies those experiences, skills and knowledge that should be offered to all young children. Specificity is necessary as there is no evidence or guarantee that, in the course of early development, all children naturally and automatically acquire the specific knowledge and skills that provide the necessary foundation for future learning.

True, given certain minimal experiences, children naturally acquire certain rudimentary skills and knowledge. For example, barring exceptional physiological or environmental conditions, all children learn to talk. However, this initial capacity for language does not automatically, in and of itself, evolve into more sophisticated language. Acquisition of a diverse vocabulary, competence in understanding and using complex grammatical structures, as well as the ability to use language symbolically, depend heavily upon the opportunity to engage in particular language experiences.

Likewise, very young children naturally acquire certain basic math concepts, recognizing, for example, quantitative differences between groups of up to four objects. However, once again, this initial natural learning does not, on its own, evolve into more advanced competencies – for example, distinguishing and counting quantities greater than four, representing the quantities with specific number words ("four") and symbols ("4"), and so on.

Readiness is not a general, all encompassing condition that simply happens naturally in the course of a child's development. Rather, children develop and achieve different levels of readiness in different content areas, based on particular experiences. A child is ready to learn new language skills on the basis of the language experiences already encountered and the skills he or she has already mastered; he or she is ready to learn certain knowledge and skills in math on the basis of the specific mathematical knowledge and skills already possessed.

Said another way, children build new learning on what they have already learned. An important component of these learning experiences is regular interaction with competent individuals who can bridge the gap between the child's existing knowledge and skills and those toward which he or she is striving.

A specific, explicit sequence of skills and knowledge, like the Core Knowledge Preschool Sequence, allows teachers, parents or other caregivers to guide a young child's development in an apprentice-like fashion, taking into account a child's particular competencies so as to offer those experiences that most closely match his or her present level, while providing the stepping stones to higher levels of competence and understanding. The child's current skills and knowledge become the starting place for new experiences and instruction, rather than a limitation or restriction.

SPECIFICITY AND PEDAGOGY

While the Preschool Sequence specifies knowledge and competencies, it does not prescribe any single pedagogy or method. In particular, it is important not to confuse or equate the precision and specificity of the Preschool Sequence goals with an approach that relies exclusively on rote learning, isolated drill, workbooks or ditto sheets.

Children learn best by participating in meaningful activities that take into account their existing competencies. The knowledge and skills specified in the Preschool Sequence may best be thought of as end goals. To reach these end goals, teachers must start "where the child is," identifying intermediate steps and activities that will, with practice over time, lead to the final goal. Often, given a child's existing competencies, the initial and intermediate steps will appropriately focus upon activities that may be described as manipulative, hands-on, concrete activities: for example, practicing patterning skills using manipulative objects like colored beads or blocks. With appropriate guidance, these concrete, hands-on activities may be gradually transformed into more abstract, representational activities. In the patterning example above, children may next be asked to use manipulative objects to reproduce or continue a pattern represented on a design or pattern card; eventually, they move to an even more abstract level, omitting entirely the use of manipulative objects, representing and creating patterns on paper only. In sum, teachers need to use a variety of methods, strategies, and materials to help children achieve the end goals described in the Preschool Sequence.

Moreover, teachers need to be aware, as pointed out by Bredekamp and Rosegrant of the National Association for the Education of Young Children (NAEYC), that "for too long, early childhood practice has been simplistically characterized as a dichotomous choice between child-centered and teacher-directed learning ... ." The most effective teachers of young children understand that at times children need to explore and discover on their own, while at other times they will make the greatest progress when a teacher intervenes in any number of ways, making the task at hand both accessible yet challenging for the young child, guiding him, step by step, to ever increasing levels of competence.

AGE GROUPINGS: LEVELS IN THE PRESCHOOL SEQUENCE

The Preschool Sequence organizes knowledge and competencies into two age groupings: Level I for 3-4 year-old children and Level II for 4-5 year-old children. These age groupings are not rigid directives but approximate guidelines based on research that, within a given area, suggests a progression of skills and knowledge. Because young children do learn at different rates, no child should be unduly rushed or held back solely based on the age groupings specified in the Preschool Sequence. The child's existing competencies in relation to the skills and knowledge of the Preschool Sequence are the best indicator of where to begin.

As noted above, the Preschool Sequence guidelines organize knowledge and skills according to two levels, ideally within the context of a two-year preschool program. The intent of this organizational design is that 3-4 year-olds first have the opportunity to participate in the Level I activities and experiences over a one-year period. The following year, these children would then build upon the foundation of the Level I experiences, moving on to Level II.

However, the reality is that, presently, many young children have at best one year of preschool experience prior to entering kindergarten. In this sense, the guidelines represent an ideal toward which we must strive. Teachers using the Preschool Sequence with 4-5 year-olds who have not had previous preschool experience must be sensitive to the possibility that there may be gaps in background experiences and knowledge that may need to be addressed before attempting certain Level II competencies. This factor must also be kept in mind when considering appropriate expectations for children in terms of mastery of the Preschool Sequence.

ASSESSMENT AND ACCOUNTABILITY

Evaluation is an integral part of good teaching practice. Assessment is an on-going process, often conducted within the context of daily experiences and activities. The teacher must start with knowledge of the child's existing competencies, relative to the end goal in question. With each subsequent activity or step taken towards the goal, he or she must evaluate the child's performance and progress to determine whether to back up, move on, change the approach, etc.

Many approaches and assessment tools already used in preschool settings, such as directed observation, checklists, work sampling and portfolios, may be adapted and used to assess children's progress relative to the Preschool Sequence.

HOW THIS BOOK RELATES TO THE SEQUENCE FOR GRADES K-8

The skills and knowledge in the Preschool Sequence are designed to correlate with the existing Core Knowledge Sequence for Grades K-8. The Preschool Sequence provides a solid, coherent foundation for the content that children will encounter in kindergarten in a school following the Core Knowledge Sequence for Grades K-8.

In a few specific instances, the Preschool Sequence overlaps the content already in the Sequence for Grades K-8. Ideally, of course, all children entering kindergarten would come prepared with the kinds of experiences and knowledge described in the Preschool Sequence. But in reality this is not the case – thus, the occasional overlap. For your reference, please note that skills or knowledge in the Preschool Sequence, also included in the Sequence for Grades K-8, are identified here by (#), with the number in the parentheses designating the grade level at which the material is included in the Sequence for Grades K-8.

DEVELOPMENT OF THE PRESCHOOL SEQUENCE

The Core Knowledge Preschool Sequence is the result of a long process of research and critical review undertaken by the non-profit Core Knowledge Foundation. The resulting Preschool Sequence represents a synthesis of exemplary practice and experience, both in the United States and abroad.

We studied the many reports that have been issued in recent years – by groups such as The Carnegie Foundation for the Advancement of Teaching, The Carnegie Corporation of New York, and The Economic and Social Research Institute – that describe the current nature of early childhood experiences for the majority of American children.

We examined important new research in cognitive development, as well as how children learn. We also examined the many documents written by professional organizations, such as the NAEYC, and government task forces at the state and national level in response to the Goals 2000 challenge to ensure that by the year 2000, all children start school ready to learn.

We looked at specific preschool practices in the United States including well-known models of early childhood education, such as Montessori, High/Scope and Creative Curriculum, as well as programs that use an eclectic approach.

We surveyed preschool practices of several other countries, including France, Japan, Korea, and Italy. The exemplary practices of the French ecoles maternelles, publicly funded French preschools that are available to all children and have been in existence for over 100 years, were selected for in-depth study. We visited classes in order to identify the common practices and experiences offered to young children; and, we examined the longitudinal research demonstrating the correlation between effective preschool experiences and their lasting, positive effects for children in all socioeconomic groups.

This wealth of information served as the basis for the development of an initial draft version of the Preschool Sequence. It is worth repeating that the programs and practices on which this draft was modeled have been empirically validated with millions of young children elsewhere in the world. (For detailed listings of specific references, see the Bibliography.)

The first draft of the Preschool Sequence was then submitted for review to nationally recognized experts in the area of early childhood development, as well as content area experts in language, emerging literacy and math. (For a list of the reviewers, see Appendix A.)

Based upon this expert review, portions of the Preschool Sequence were modified and this new draft of the Preschool Sequence was field tested in 1996-1997 in several preschool settings, representing both full-day and half-day programs. During the same period, this working draft was distributed throughout the United States to early childhood specialists, administrators, preschool and kindergarten teachers for public comment. The draft was also presented for discussion at the 1997 National Core Knowledge Conference.

Using feedback from these many sources, refinements were made to clarify the material presented in the guidelines and to offer practical suggestions for implementation. The present Core Knowledge Preschool Sequence is the result of these many efforts.

Common Questions
About the Core Knowledge Preschool Sequence

What is "Core Knowledge?"

The "Core Knowledge" movement is an educational reform based on the premise that a grade-by-grade core of common learnings is necessary to ensure a sound and fair elementary education. The movement was started by Dr. E.D. Hirsch, Jr., author of *Cultural Literacy* and *The Schools We Need*, and is based on a large body of research in cognitive psychology and comparative research of the world's fairest and most effective school systems. Dr. Hirsch has argued that for the sake of academic excellence, greater fairness and higher literacy, early schooling should provide a solid, specific, shared core curriculum in order to help children establish strong foundations of knowledge. After wide consultation, the content of this core curriculum has been outlined in grade-by-grade guides – the Core Knowledge Preschool Sequence and the Core Knowledge Sequence, K-8 – that state explicitly the knowledge to be presented at each level. Currently, hundreds of schools and thousands of dedicated educators are participating in this school reform movement throughout the United States.

What is the Core Knowledge Foundation and what resources or services can it provide?

The Core Knowledge Foundation is an independent, nonprofit and nonpartisan organization founded in 1986 by Dr. E.D. Hirsch, Jr. Dr. Hirsch receives no remuneration from the Foundation or from the book royalties it generates. We conduct research on curricula, develop books and other materials for parents and teachers, and serve as a hub of communications between schools using Core Knowledge.

We can provide a variety of publications, including introductory general information packets about Core Knowledge. The Core Knowledge Preschool Sequence, as well as the Core Knowledge Sequence, K-8 and other publications can be ordered directly from the Foundation. If you become a member of the Core Knowledge Network, you will also receive a quarterly newsletter.

We can put you in touch with people at experienced Core Knowledge schools. You can begin by checking out the Core Knowledge Home Page at http://www.coreknowledge.org. There you'll find links to Core Knowledge schools and information about Core-Net, a helpful place to share ideas, lessons and resources.

The Core Knowledge Foundation also offers a variety of staff development workshops to help ensure successful implementation of the Core Knowledge program in your school. We will be happy to plan a complete training program to meet your school's particular needs. Please call the Foundation for further information about scheduling and cost.

We also hold an annual national conference, usually during the month of March, that provides many opportunities for idea-sharing and extended networking. Check our home page or call the Foundation for specific dates and location.

What does it mean to be a "Core Knowledge School?" Does every teacher need to be involved?

Some individual teachers select parts of Core Knowledge to teach. While the Core Knowledge Foundation encourages these teachers in their efforts, we see this undertaking as just the beginning of the larger process of a whole school deciding to become a Core Knowledge school.

At a Core Knowledge school, the grade-level topics are not viewed as resources to pick and choose from, but as the common ground upon which a faculty meets and collaborates to teach a sequenced, coherent curriculum. In this cumulative curriculum, the knowledge and skills learned each year become the foundation for learning in subsequent years.

It is not absolutely necessary, at first, that all teachers use the Core Knowledge program, though the ultimate goal is involvement of all teachers. Some schools begin by taking the plunge and getting all teachers involved in Core Knowledge from the outset. But successful implementation can begin with a core of interested and committed teachers. Some schools have successfully implemented Core Knowledge beginning at one grade level, then adding successive grade levels.

As more teachers get involved, there tends to be more enthusiasm and, most important, more collaboration. The most successful Core Knowledge schools are those in which teachers work together to share ideas, resources, and lesson plans.

There are now hundreds of Core Knowledge schools throughout the country and the number continues to grow. The Core Knowledge Preschool Sequence is the most recent addition to Core Knowledge. Many Core Knowledge elementary schools with pre-kindergarten classes are now in the process of adding this component to their programs.

How does the Core Knowledge Preschool Sequence relate to the Core Knowledge Sequence, K-8?

An underlying principle of Core Knowledge is that we acquire new knowledge by building on what we already know. Core Knowledge advocates a curriculum that is explicitly designed to present a coherent sequence of skills and knowledge that build cumulatively year by year. Thus, each level of the Core Knowledge Sequence begins by extending and developing what has been learned at the previous levels. The skills and knowledge of the Preschool Sequence provide a solid foundation for the content that children will encounter in a good kindergarten, for instance one in a school that follows the Core Knowledge Sequence.

While it is hoped that children who use the Core Knowledge Preschool Sequence will continue to pursue a content-rich program in a Core Knowledge elementary school, the Preschool Sequence will, in any case, provide a sound basis for success in non-Core Knowledge kindergartens as well.

Our preschool already has a "program." Why change what we're already doing?

Many preschools that already have a "program" find, on close examination, that what they have is not a definite curriculum with specific goals for young children, but instead a general set of theoretical beliefs that focus on how children learn, rather than what they need to learn.

The Core Knowledge Preschool Sequence identifies skill and knowledge competencies in all areas – Physical Well-Being and Motor Development, Social and Emotional Development, Approaches to Learning, Language Development, Knowledge Acquisition and Cognitive Development. By specifying definite expectations, the Core Knowledge Preschool Sequence provides everyone – teachers, parents and children – with a clear vision of where they are going. Knowing these definite goals allows teachers to provide experiences that will lead children toward their acquisition.

Setting clear expectations and standards has repeatedly proven to be the most effective way of ensuring that all young children gain the knowledge and skills they need for future learning in school.

Is the Core Knowledge Preschool Sequence developmentally appropriate?

Over the past ten years, the term developmentally appropriate has been used by many people to mean many things. The National Association for the Education of Young Children (NAEYC), which originally coined the phrase developmentally appropriate practice, issued a revised position statement in 1997 in order to clarify the misinterpretations of the term. This revised position statement takes into account current understanding of how the brain develops and how young children learn. In many ways, the description of developmentally appropriate practice in this new NAEYC document differs significantly from what many in the field have called developmentally appropriate practice over the years. It is still unclear whether the early childhood field as a whole has a common understanding of what developmentally appropriate practice is, as put forth in the NAEYC document. One must therefore interpret with caution the use of this term without further explanation. (For a more thorough examination of the two position statements on developmentally appropriate practice issued by NAEYC, see Appendix B, *Ten Years Later: Developmentally Appropriate Practice – What Have We Learned?*)

What we can say with confidence is that the Core Knowledge Preschool Sequence is developmentally appropriate. It is modeled on programs and practices that have been empirically validated with millions of young children elsewhere in the world. For example, in France, where public preschool programs have been available to all young children for over the past 100 years, there are standards like the Core Knowledge ones that guide the program offered to all preschoolers. Certain learnings are so important to every child's social, emotional, cognitive, physical and academic development that they warrant explicit specification and intervention to ensure that they are a part of every child's preschool years.

How can you expect all children to learn the same material when all children are unique, with particular abilities, rates of development, interests and learning styles? Shouldn't educational goals and content be individualized for each child on the basis of these individual differences?

For academic excellence and social justice, it is important to have high expectations and goals for all young children. Of course, the strategies and techniques that teachers use to help each child achieve these goals may differ, taking into account each child's unique abilities, learning style, and so on. However, in recent years, educators have taken this view to extremes. The highly respected Carnegie Corporation addressed this issue in its report, *Years of Promise: A Comprehensive Learning Strategy for America's Children* (1996):

> "This belief (in difference and uniqueness) is simply wrong. When it is applied to whole groups of children on the basis of language, race or ethnicity, it is not only wrong, it is racist. The fact is that differences among children predict little about what they will be able to achieve, when they have the right motivation, attention and support. . . . Overcoming dangerous myths about children's aptitudes . . . means expecting all children to master the same ambitious content while recognizing that individual children will progress by different routes and at different rates."

What about children whose native language is other than standard English?

Considerable emphasis in the Core Knowledge Preschool Sequence is placed on the development of everyday and academic language skills. It has a unique guide to the "language of instruction" for young children. This strong emphasis on language in the Preschool Sequence is consistent with the importance of early language development for future learning.

It is especially important that those children who come to preschool with a native language other than standard English be offered the opportunity to learn and master the language competencies included in the Preschool Sequence. Rich language experiences at the preschool level can significantly enhance a young child's chances for success as he enters kindergarten and more formal schooling. We also know that, as a result of the brain development process, children are most capable of easily learning a second language when they are young. Of course, preschool teachers should recognize that children for whom English is not a native language may need special attention.

Is the Core Knowledge Preschool Sequence a compensatory program only for disadvantaged children?

Absolutely not. The Core Knowledge Preschool Sequence will provide a solid foundation for future learning for all young children. Historically, it is true that disadvantaged children as a group have been frequently subjected to mediocre educational practice. The explicit specification of what is to be taught, as contained in the Preschool Sequence, safeguards all children against the likelihood of lower expectations and watered down curricula. Research clearly documents the positive benefits of a preschool education guided by standards for all children, regardless of socioeconomic level and family background.

Okay, I'm interested in the Core Knowledge Preschool Sequence. What's next?

Begin by becoming familiar with all sections of the Core Knowledge Preschool Sequence. Share copies of the Preschool Sequence with other members of your school – administrators, teachers and parents - and set aside time to compare the Core Knowledge Preschool Sequence with what you are already doing, as well as with existing state or local guidelines for preschoolers. It is important to take time to answer questions and build understanding among members of your school community, so that there can be a shared effort to make Core Knowledge succeed. If your conversations lead to a consensus – "We want to implement the Core Knowledge Preschool Sequence" – then it's time to move on to more in-depth planning. Such planning will include developing a month-by-month planning guide that integrates the Core Knowledge Preschool Sequence content and competencies with any existing programs and district/state guidelines, assessing present material resources, involving parents and the community in obtaining other needed resources, etc.

Do we have to teach everything that is listed in the Core Knowledge Preschool Sequence?

The goal is to teach all of the Preschool Sequence. But the first year or two of implementation, teachers may need to phase in the various components of the Sequence to accommodate their own needs for professional development, as well as the acquisition and development of resources. For example, perhaps a particular preschool presently has neither the instrumental musical selections nor art prints specified in the Music and Visual Arts sections of the Preschool Sequence, nor the financial resources to purchase all of these materials at the same time. A decision might be made to purchase the musical materials during the first year and fully implement the Music component of the Sequence, while delaying purchase of the art prints until the coming year. The particular visual arts competencies that focus on specific works of art would then be phased in during the second year of implementation.

What does it mean to be an official Core Knowledge preschool? What does my school or class need to do to be a Core Knowledge Preschool?

There are certain criteria that a preschool center or preschool class (within an elementary school setting) must meet in order to be considered an official Core Knowledge preschool. These include developing a year long month-by-month guide to teach the Preschool Sequence, developing representative lesson plans for each area of the of the Preschool Sequence and demonstrating a certain level of implementation. The first step in this process is to complete a "Preschool Profile" with information about your school. A preschool center or class may do this as soon as they begin to implement the Preschool Sequence. Contact the Core Knowledge Foundation, 804-977-7550, to obtain a Preschool Profile or more information.

The Core Knowledge Preschool Sequence is divided into two levels: Level I for three/four year-olds and Level II for four/five year-olds. Our school just has one year of preschool, made up of four year-olds who will go on to kindergarten the following year. Where should we start, Level I or II? What if some children are not ready for Level II? Should we wait until they are ready?

Given the Core Knowledge premise that each subsequent year's skills and knowledge build upon those acquired previously, certainly the ideal situation is one in which 4-5 year-old children have already participated in experiences and activities that have led to the acquisition of the knowledge and competencies specified in Level I of the Preschool Sequence. In reality, that may or may not be the case for the particular children in your class. However, the notion of simply waiting until children become ready is outdated and ineffective. Children develop and achieve readiness based on the opportunities and experiences with which they are presented.

As a preschool teacher, you have to start somewhere. If you do have just a single year preschool program with 4-5 year-olds, we suggest that you still start with the Level II competencies within each area of the Preschool Sequence. Carefully monitor the children's progress. If individuals or groups of children have difficulty, check the related competencies in Level I of the Sequence and recognize that you may need to back up and provide missing prior experiences.

For example, perhaps you are playing a game that involves catching a large ball, a Level II competency from the "Movement and Coordination" section of the Sequence. If some children experience difficulty, frequently dropping the ball, you may want to look at the analogous Level I competency in "Movement and Coordination" and then give these children the opportunity to play their own game using a beanbag, instead of a ball.

Keep in mind, however, that this does not necessarily mean that these same children will always need to drop back to the Level I competencies in all areas of the Sequence; perhaps some of these same children have had rich experiences with nursery rhymes, poems and so on and are ready to start out immediately with the Level II competencies in this area.

How can I assess the progress of my students relative to the competencies and knowledge specified in the Core Knowledge Preschool Sequence?

The question of how to assess Core Knowledge is part of the larger discussion about assessment in schools today. This discussion currently focuses on a perceived tension between authentic assessments and standardized assessments. The Core Knowledge Foundation sees this discussion as falsely polarized, making opposites out of what should be complementary initiatives. There is merit in both forms of assessment when they are used for the purposes for which each is best suited.

When considering individual students in a particular class, evaluation of each student's progress is an indispensable part of effective teaching. Such assessment is an on-going process, often conducted within the context of daily experiences and activities. This form of authentic assessment may be carried out using such teacher tools as directed observation, checklists, work sampling, portfolios and selected activity probes. This type of assessment is reliable and valid only when two key considerations are clearly specified: what is being assessed in terms of children's work and the criteria used to determine satisfactory or unsatisfactory performance. The specificity of the competencies of the Core Knowledge Preschool Sequence facilitates systematic and deliberate use of authentic assessment devices to monitor each child's progress. Teachers are encouraged to use the Preschool Sequence to guide their observations and collections of student work, as well as to develop activity probes as needed to assess mastery.

At the same time, the data derived from standardized testing is useful in assessing the effectiveness or performance of a school (as opposed to individual children), program or methodology. When used for this purpose, standardized test data enables teachers and administrators to critically examine current practices and to ensure that the end results are those which were desired.

Unfortunately, until very recently, the value and purpose of standardized testing at the early childhood level was so little appreciated and understood that little initiative was taken to develop well-made standardized tests that were also simple and efficient to administer to preschoolers. Few reliable and valid group-administered tests currently exist that would simply and effectively evaluate the breadth and depth of the knowledge and skills included in the Preschool Sequence. Some individually administered, existing tests are appropriate, but may require special training to administer as well as a considerable investment of class time. As parents and educators continue to call for increasing accountability, it is hoped that more effective and efficient means of standardized assessment will be forthcoming.

What kinds of preschool settings can use the Core Knowledge Preschool Sequence? What about half day programs?

The Core Knowledge Preschool Sequence may be used by interested individuals to guide the planning and provision of experiences and activities for young children in a variety of settings, including public and private preschool or pre-kindergarten programs, center or home based day care programs, Head Start, etc. The single most important factor to consider in deciding whether or not to implement the Preschool Sequence is whether there is a commitment by those who will use the Sequence to fully study, understand and integrate it into their daily activities.

As far as full vs. half day programs, the Core Knowledge Preschool Sequence has been used effectively in both.

Does the explicit specification of skills and competencies in the Core Knowledge Preschool Sequence mean that a teacher-directed approach to instruction is best? What about discovery learning and child-initiated activities?

As previously noted, Core Knowledge specifies what to teach, not how to teach, and so, no one single teaching method is necessarily best. As is the case with many educational issues, any practice that tends towards an either-or approach has the ring of extremism and inaccuracy – "Only knowledge and skills presented through structured, teacher-directed activities will be truly mastered by young children" is just as misleading as "Children will be most receptive to acquiring new knowledge and skills if they are encouraged to explore and discover on their own."

The most effective teachers understand that they have a wide-ranging continuum of teaching approaches from which to choose at any given time. Sometimes it may be most effective and appropriate to present a concept or skill or do an activity in a small group, planned and directed by the teacher. Alternatively, children may play and work independently in centers of their own choosing, or they may play and work in centers that have been selected with the teacher's guidance. The goal is to help each child progress to increasing skill, mastery and autonomy in performing the Preschool Sequence competencies – to provide challenging, but not frustrating, learning experiences.

Everybody is talking about preschoolers' lack of readiness for academic activities when they enter kindergarten, especially in the area of reading. I'm confused – some people say that preschoolers should not be forced to learn letters and others say the most important way to prepare children to read is to teach them the names of all the letters of the alphabet. Who's

right? Does the Core Knowledge Preschool Sequence specify that all preschoolers be able to identify all the letters of the alphabet by name?

Our understanding of the early reading process has dramatically increased in recent years thanks to greater awareness of reading research. [See *Beginning to Read: Thinking and Learning about Print – A Summary* by Marilyn Jager Adams (1990) and *Preventing Reading Difficulties in Young Children* by Catherine Snow, Susan Burns and Peg Griffin (1998).] We now know that early reading facility is influenced and enhanced by competency in a number of skills, one of which is recognition of the alphabetic code, that is, the identification of letters. Learning letter names has traditionally been viewed as the first, and sometimes only, step taken towards reading preparation at the preschool level.

We know now that other skills, in addition to knowing letter names, are also important. Among these skills is something called "phonemic awareness," the ability to listen to spoken language and discriminate sounds, breaking words apart into sounds and then putting them back together. "Print awareness" is also important – knowing how and why print is used, what a letter or word is, and so on. Developing an understanding of "story structure or schema" as something with different characters, a setting and a beginning, middle and end, also plays a role in beginning reading development.

This new understanding of the reading process has helped us recognize that many preliminary pre-reading skills must come together before a child can successfully tackle the complex task of reading. Development of just one of these skills during the preschool years, without the others, will not adequately prepare a child for the challenges that lie ahead in kindergarten and first grade. Therefore, the Core Knowledge Preschool Sequence addresses each of the many skills that research has determined are important to early reading.

One of these skills is learning to recognize and identify letters by name. However, in an effort to be sure that this is not the only pre-reading skill taught to preschoolers, the Preschool Sequence specifies a limited number of letters that preschoolers are expected to know, allowing time for the development of phonemic awareness, print awareness and story schema, as well. Some preschoolers will be capable of doing all of this and learning all the letters; they should be encouraged to do so. However a basic or minimum goal for all preschoolers should be to learn some letters, along with the other skills.

Doesn't a curriculum such as Core Knowledge, that specifies what is to be taught at the pre-school and each subsequent grade level, limit the creativity of teachers?

Like educational policy and practice in most developed nations, such as France, Germany and Japan, Core Knowledge does identify specific standards, or what is to be taught, at each grade level. Certain knowledge and skills are deemed so important as to warrant ensuring each child's access to such knowledge and skills through explicit specification as standards.

It is important to make a distinction, however, between specifying what is to be taught at a particular grade level as compared to how it is to be taught. Teachers at Core Knowledge schools report that the curricular guidelines that specify what is to be taught are not restricting, but liberating and empowering. Given a baseline of what to teach, teachers are free to devote their creative energies to developing innovative, stimulating lessons that use a wide variety of teaching approaches.

I still have other questions about what certain parts of the Preschool Sequence mean and how to implement them. What can I do?

Please feel free to contact Linda Bevilacqua, Director of the Early Childhood Core Knowledge Program either by phone (804-977-7550) or e-mail (lindab@coreknowledge.org) for further assistance. You might also want to inquire on Core-Net, the Core Knowledge list server on the Internet.

Organizational Note

Throughout the Preschool Sequence, goals and competencies are presented according to two levels. Content, including specific vocabulary, which is included within the actual goals, should be considered part of the core competency and should be presented to all children.

For many goals, an example or note is often included in a separate column to provide further clarification. The included examples are but a sample of many possibilities. Teachers may choose to translate the example provided into an actual instructional experience or they may instead generate other instructional possibilities.

1
Movement
and
Coordination

Movement and Coordination

OVERVIEW: This section describes motor and coordination skills, and related movement activities that extend and refine notions of body image and the body's capabilities. It also provides opportunities for enhancing time, space, and language concepts, as well as social development (when activities are carried out with others).

The basic goals ask the child to stop and start movement according to a signal, maintain balance, move through space, with or without obstacles, in a variety of ways, throw and kick objects, and move cooperatively with others, through a variety of tasks or traditional childhood games. The child is also asked to use the body to interpret music and to perform pantomimes.

Goal: Refine Physical Attention and Relaxation

	LEVEL I	LEVEL II
EXAMPLE: Stop and/or start movement: *visual signal* - flag waving; *auditory signal* - whistle.	• Stop and/or start movement and physical activity in response to a visual or auditory signal.	• Relax specific body muscles and/or the whole body, moving from a high activity level to a quiet, focused state.

Goal: Develop and Refine Gross Motor Skills

	LEVEL I	LEVEL II
	• Ascend and descend steps, alternating feet.	
EXAMPLE: standing on one foot, stooping, reaching, etc.	• Maintain balance: changing body position without moving through space.	
	• Maintain balance: walking forward on a wide bench or beam.	• Maintain balance: walking forward, backward and sideways on a balance beam, 10" wide or less.
EXAMPLE: inside cartons of different sizes, tunnels, tires, hoops; under a table or bench; within the boundaries of a shape outlined on the ground.	• Situate oneself within a space of defined boundaries, modifying body configuration and size to "fit the space."	
EXAMPLE: ascend and descend (ladders and climbing apparatus), climb (up an incline), roll or slide (down an incline), crawl (under a bench), somersault (around a low bar), jump (from a beam/bench to a mat; from one hoop to the next).	• Move through space with or without obstacles, without touching or bumping into other individuals or obstacles, by: crawling, walking, running, galloping, hopping (same foot and alternate foot) or jumping.	• Move through space with obstacles, using various movements to surmount the obstacles by: ascending and descending, climbing, rolling, sliding, crawling, somersaulting, jumping.
		• Complete a circuit or obstacle course, following arrows or the path indicated.

Goal: Develop and Refine Eye-Hand and Eye-Foot Coordination Skills

LEVEL I	LEVEL II
• Throw or kick an object in the direction indicated.	• Throw or kick an object with increasing accuracy at identified targets, that vary in height and distance.
• Play "catch" with a bean bag with a partner, seated or standing 1½ feet apart.	• Play "catch" with a large ball with a partner, seated or standing 2½ feet apart.
	• Ride a tricycle.
	• Maintain momentum on a swing by "pumping legs."
• Coordinate motor activity to carry out a goal with a partner or group: push a large, heavy object from one location to another.	• Coordinate motor activity to carry out a goal with a partner or group: carry a large object from one location to another.

Goal: Play Group Games

LEVEL I	LEVEL II
• Participate in group games, such as the following: Farmer in the Dell, Follow the Leader, Hot Potato, London Bridge, Mother May I, Ring Around the Rosie, Simon Says.	• Participate in group games, such as the following: Duck, Duck, Goose, Drop the Handkerchief, Kitty Wants a Corner, Musical Chairs, Red Light/ Green Light, Relay Race, Tag and variations.

Goal: Use the Body Expressively

LEVEL I	LEVEL II
• Imitate the position or action of another person.	
• Act out a simple pantomime (a person performing a single activity, an animal, etc.).	• Act out a nursery rhyme, poem or fingerplay.
	• Move to music.

NOTE: See Music for specific competencies.

Language of Instruction

ALSO: See Language of
Instruction for Orientation in
Space (positional words) and
Autonomy and Social Skills (body
image vocabulary).

NOTE: For a full discussion,
please see "Language of
Instruction," in the Preschool
Sequence Introduction and in
the Implementation section.

TEACHER AND CHILDREN		TEACHER ONLY	
catch		act out	sideways
climb		aim	signal
dance		backward	slide
fast		balance	somersault
jump		crawl	speed
kick		forward	still
loud		gallop	suspend
move		hop	target
quiet		imitate	tricycle
run		incline	pantomime
slow		interpret	play catch
soft		ladder	pump legs
start		moving	relax
stop		obstacle	relay race
throw		obstacle course	roll
walk		rules	

EXAMPLE: Use vocabulary from
the Movement and Coordination
section as follows:

ADULT: I want to see how many different ways you can *move* down this (pointing) *incline*. Who can show me one way to move down the *incline*?
> *Child rolls down incline*

ADULT: Good – you can *roll sideways* down the *incline*. What's another way?
> *Child crawls down incline*

ADULT: Right – you can *crawl* down the *incline* on your hands and knees, etc.

2
Autonomy
and
Social Skills

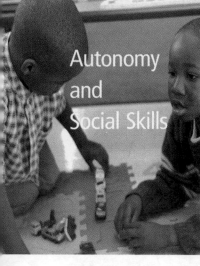

Autonomy and Social Skills

OVERVIEW: The basic goals associated with this section focus on the development of those emotional and social skills that enable the young child to function independently within the social setting of the class group. These include developing a sense of who he or she is and his or her capacities, beginning with a sense of physical body image. The child will also learn those interpersonal, social skills essential to interacting with others, such as the "give and take" of being part of a group and the need to sometimes delay or defer his or her own immediate desires, given the demands of the group. These goals mark the beginning development of an individual who is independent and competent, able to assume responsibility for his or her actions within the context of the group.

Goal: Establish a Sense of Self and Personal Responsibility

LEVEL I	LEVEL II
• Recognize and respond to own first and last name, orally and in writing.	
• When asked, orally provide first and last name.	
• Internalize and conceptualize an image of one's body: • identify and name the following body parts: head, hair, eye, eyebrow, eyelash, ear, nose, forehead, mouth, lip, tongue, teeth, cheek, chin, face, neck, shoulder, arm, elbow, wrist, hand, finger, nail, chest, back, stomach, waist, hip, leg, knee, ankle, foot, toe, heel, body.	• Internalize and conceptualize an image of one's body:
• draw a simple line drawing of a person, such as a stick figure, that includes a head, with eyes, nose, mouth, body, arms and legs.	• draw a dimensional picture of a person that includes a head, with eyes, eyebrows, nose, mouth, hair, neck, body, arms with hands, legs with feet.
• Care for personal needs: • practice good hygiene (use bathroom independently, wash hands, etc.)	• Care for personal needs:
• demonstrate appropriate table manners (feed self, using fork, spoon and knife, appropriate use of napkin, etc.)	
• dress self independently, putting on clothing.	• dress self independently, fastening clothing, using buttons and zippers.

Goal: Function and Work Constructively in a Group Setting, Using Appropriate Social Skills

LEVEL I	LEVEL II
• Identify other members of the group: recognize and call by name classmates (first name) and teacher (Mr./Mrs./Ms).	• Identify other members of the group: recognize, call by name (Mr./Mrs./Ms.) and indicate the role of other school personnel.

Goal: Function and Work Constructively in a Group Setting, Using Appropriate Social Skills, continued

LEVEL I	LEVEL II
• Use verbal, social forms of politeness: • acknowledge and return greetings and farewells, such as, good morning, hello, hi, good-bye, etc.	
• greet adults as Mr., Mrs., or Ms. (name).	
• make requests and acknowledge attempts to meet requests politely, such as, please, thank you, no, thank you, you're welcome, etc.	
• Carry out certain chores that contribute to the well-being and functioning of the group.	• Carry out certain chores that contribute to the well-being and functioning of the group.
• Follow accepted rules for group behavior: • attend and listen during a group activity while others speak.	
	• Follow accepted rules for group behavior: • interrupt a conversation between two people politely.
• wait turn to speak in a group, using agreed upon signals.	• ask appropriately for the help of an adult when needed.
	• offer assistance to another child.
• sit among other children during a group activity, remaining in own physical space without disrupting or interfering with others.	• respect the personal belongings/property of others.
• given advance notice, stop when told and change activities, moving smoothly and cooperatively from one activity to another.	• take turns using toys, share materials.
• follow the rules for simple childhood games (board games and group circle games).	• follow the rules for simple childhood games (board games and group circle games).
	• accept consequences of actions, either positive or negative.
	• attempt to solve problems and/or conflicts using words.

EXAMPLE: help set table, distribute the snack, empty the trash can, wipe up spills, sweep the floor, etc.

EXAMPLE: waiting to be acknowledged, standing apart from and not between the two individuals who are speaking, saying excuse me, etc.

EXAMPLE: raising hand and waiting for acknowledgment from the teacher; being called by name, a nod, eye contact.

EXAMPLE: Candyland, Lotto Games, Simon Says, Musical Chairs, etc.

EXAMPLE: accepts a compliment; or, apologizes and attempts to correct an inappropriate action/situation ("I'm sorry").

Language of Instruction

NOTE: For a full discussion, please see "Language of Instruction," in the Preschool Sequence Introduction and in the Implementation section.

TEACHER AND CHILDREN		TEACHER ONLY	
BODY PARTS	SOCIAL SKILLS	BODY PARTS	SOCIAL SKILLS
ankle	excuse me	part(s)	apologize
arm	good morning		interrupt
back	good-bye		
body	hello		
cheek	hi		
chest	Mr.		
chin	Mrs.		
ear	Ms.		
elbow	no, thank you		
eye	please		
eyebrow	sorry		
eyelash	thank you		
face	yes, please		
feet	you're welcome		
finger			
forehead			
foot			
hair			
hand			
head			
heel			
hip			
knee			
leg			
lip			
mouth			
nail			
neck			
nose			
shoulder			
stomach			
teeth			
toe			
tongue			
tooth			
waist			
wrist			

EXAMPLE: Use vocabulary from the Autonomy and Social Skills section as follows:

CHILD: I made a picture.

ADULT: Let's see. What can you tell me about your picture?

CHILD: It's me.

ADULT: Ahh, you drew a picture of yourself. Can you tell me about the different *parts* of the drawing – the different *parts* of the *body*, what is this (points to *head*)?

CHILD: The *head*.

ADULT: You drew a picture of a *head*. And where is your *head*? Point to your *head*. That's right. Now tell me about the different parts of the *head* you drew. Where are the *eyebrows*? Are these the *eyebrows*?

3

Work
Habits

Work Habits

OVERVIEW: The foundation for the manner in which children will later approach academic work in kindergarten and beyond is established, step by step, through the experiences and expectations that children encounter in play and activities at the preschool level. This section focuses on gently guiding children to develop a methodology for approaching different activities, to develop memory skills, follow directions, persist at a task, identify the materials and steps needed to carry out an activity, evaluate and correct their own work, and so on.

Goal: **Develop Memorization Skills**

LEVEL I	LEVEL II
	• Memorize address (street, city and state), phone number and date of birth (month and day).

NOTE: See also Nursery Rhymes, Poems, Songs and Fingerplays, for developing memory skills.

Goal: **Develop Independent Work Habits**

LEVEL I	LEVEL II
• Carry out oral directions: single-step directions.	
	• Carry out oral directions: multi-step directions, accompanied by a preliminary demonstration.

EXAMPLE: Draw small circles inside the box.

EXAMPLE: (See note below.)
To make your own Valentine's Day card, first trace the heart shape, using the stencil, on the front of the card. Then, squeeze and scrunch together each piece of colored tissue paper to make a small ball. Dab each ball in a bit of glue and place it on the inside of the heart shape until it is completely covered and you can't see any white space. When you finish the heart, open your card, copy the words, "I love you" and then write your name.

NOTE:
This example of multi-step directions is an "end goal." To achieve this level of competency, young children will need many opportunities for practice with intermediate steps and prompts. For example, the teacher might begin with simpler, shorter multi-step directions.

• Given a choice of several familiar toys/activities, choose one and use it independently for a sustained period of time: at least 10 minutes (if the activity has a definite end, i.e., a puzzle, craft, etc., continue until complete, even if less than 10 minutes).	• Given a choice of several familiar toys/activities, choose one and use it independently for a sustained period of time: at least 20 minutes (if the activity has a definite end, i.e., a puzzle, craft, etc., continue until complete, even if less than 20 minutes).

NOTE: Keep in mind that the designated durations of sustained activity are "end goals." To achieve the level of competency indicated for each level, young children will need many opportunities to practice and complete tasks of shorter duration, building progressively to the end goal.

Goal: Develop Independent Work Habits, continued

LEVEL I	LEVEL II
• Return toys/materials to their proper location after use.	• Return toys/materials to their proper location after use.
• Once initiated, work in an orderly, persistent fashion in completing a task with a definite end (art or craft project, puzzle, etc.), even if difficulty is encountered or several "sessions" are needed.	• Once initiated, work in an orderly, persistent fashion in completing a task with a definite end (art or craft project, puzzle, etc.), even if difficulty is encountered or several "sessions" are needed.
	• With the assistance of an adult as needed, organize and plan what is needed to carry out a project or task: materials, tools, process (what steps and what techniques.).
EXAMPLE: Compare construction of a multicolored, wooden bead necklace, bead by bead, with a pattern card to determine if necklace matches pattern.	• With the assistance and feedback of an adult as needed, describe and evaluate own work, identify and correct errors, refine work.

Language of Instruction

TEACHER AND CHILDREN	TEACHER ONLY

NOTE: For a full discussion, please see "Language of Instruction," in the Preschool Sequence Introduction and in the Implementation section.

INDEPENDENT WORK HABITS

correct
effort
error
follow directions
independently
materials
mistake
persevere
responsibility
tools

MEMORIZATION

attention
concentrate
memorize
remember

EXAMPLE: Use vocabulary from the Work Habits section as follows:

CHILD: Uh oh! The milk spilled. It's a big mess.

ADULT: Oops, there was an accident and the milk spilled. That's okay – sometimes accidents happen. Sometimes we make *mistakes* – everyone does. But now there is a mess. Let's see – what do we need to do with the mess? What do we need to do to fix or *correct* what happened?

CHILD: Clean it up.

ADULT: That's right. And when we make a mess or spill something, it's our *responsibility* to clean it up – that means that it's our job to clean it up. I'll help you by getting the sponge for you and then you can be *responsible* for wiping up the milk (hands child the sponge). Do you know how to wipe up the milk or should I show you how to get started?

Language Development
Introduction

Language Development **Introduction**

It is almost impossible to overemphasize the significance of early language development and its impact upon nearly every aspect of future development. We live in a culture in which, in a very real sense, an individual's ability to "use language" is synonymous with the ability to think. Words and the way that they may be linked together in sentences to express and relate ideas provide the lens or filters through which we perceive, understand and analyze our world and experiences.

In identifying competencies that fall under the general category of language, it is useful to consider several different dimensions of language – the function versus the form of language; receptive vs. expressive language; and oral vs. written language.

Certain language skills fall under the function category addressing the various purposes or ways in which language is used.

Language may be used as a form of discourse, a means of personal and interpersonal communication. Subcategories can be further identified:
- Conversing – carrying on a simple conversation
- Asserting State of Being, Needs and Desires – describing physical sensations, mental states or emotional feelings, " I want ..." or "I need...," etc.
- Narrating – describing an object, person, event or experience
- Explaining/Directing – giving directions or instructions, often step by step
- Expressing a Point of View/Imagining – giving an opinion, pretending and assuming the role or perspective of another, making up a story.

In addition, language may be used to symbolically represent concrete objects and actual experiences in order to organize, relate and analyze information – in short, for thinking. Several subcategories include:
- Predicting – anticipating and saying what is likely to happen next
- Relating Concepts/Thinking Logically – giving opposites, sorting and classifying, relating cause and effect.

Other language skills associated with the form of language are those that address the structure or the nuts and bolts of language. In addition to mastering the sounds and pronunciation of words, a skill that most young children will have accomplished in the early toddler years, preschoolers must also build:
- Vocabulary – acquiring increasingly precise and varied ways to express nuances of meaning
- Syntax – learning the grammar of language word order in a sentence, word endings to reflect singular and plural, past and present, as well as specific ways of connecting words and phrases that indicate different relationships, cause-effect, temporal, etc.

In addition, language may be characterized as receptive language, i.e., comprehension, or expressive language, i.e., production. Development does not necessarily proceed at a parallel pace between these two language dimensions. Generally, receptive language precedes expressive language. Said another way, children need to understand and comprehend language before being expected to produce language; for example, children need many opportunities to listen to narrative descriptions (in adult commentary, story books and so on) before they can be expected to produce narrative descriptions themselves.

Finally, language may be described as oral (spoken) language or written language, symbolically represented by various combinations of the letters of the alphabet in the form of written words and sentences. In terms of language development, the primary focus during the preschool years is, of course, on oral language development; however, it is also important to recognize that, given appropriate experiences, the initial foundation for written language development is also put into place at this time.

The four segments of the Preschool Sequence that follow address each of these language dimensions. While conceptually organized in four separate sections, Oral Language; Nursery Rhymes, Poems, Fingerplays and Songs; Storybook Reading and Storytelling; and Emerging Literacy Skills in Reading and Writing, the language skills in each section are closely interrelated, building upon and reinforcing the competencies found in the other sections.

To aid teachers and caregivers in seeing these interrelationships in language skills, the competencies in each section have been cross-referenced according to the various subcategories listed in this introduction.

4

Oral
Language

Oral Language

OVERVIEW: The basic goals in this section focus on understanding and using spoken language through the development of basic conversational skills, as well as more complex discourse skills: clearly communicating one's needs, understanding or giving a verbal description of a person, object or experience, sequencing the events of a particular experience in chronological order, giving directions or explaining how to do something, offering a personal opinion, using pretend language, and so on. Children benefit from many experiences and opportunities to listen and talk in a variety of circumstances, moving from using language in strictly contextualized situations, referring to objects or events present in the immediate environment, to using decontextualized language, moving beyond the here and now. Language can then be used symbolically – to talk about the past, answer "what if" questions, link cause and effect, as well as to conceptually sort and classify. Additional goals in this section address mastering the form of oral language, both vocabulary and syntax.

While it is beyond the intended purpose of the Preschool Sequence to provide suggestions and activities on how to teach the listed competencies, it is particularly important in this section on oral language to emphasize the teaching of these skills within the context of learning opportunities, in the form of child-adult interactions and conversations, that present themselves continuously on a daily basis. The manner in which adults respond to children's utterances and the subsequent opportunities offered for additional conversation and talk clearly influence children's language development.

Language research suggests that children benefit from:
- Frequent language interaction, with many opportunities to listen and talk.
- Adult models of high quality talk, that keep in mind children's need to first hear many "language examples" in order to build a receptive language base: use of a variety of vocabulary, including occasional "rare words" (multi-syllable words that might normally be considered "outside a preschooler's vocabulary"), use of a variety of syntactical forms such as complex sentences that relate ideas, talk that is informative and illustrates reflection and problem solving, etc.
- Adult responses that reflect and incorporate what the child has said but also expand upon his or her comments.
- Adult comments and behaviors that invite further conversation on the child's part: a question, a pause (after a question, allowing several seconds of quiet time for the child to process the question), a rise in intonation of the voice, a facial expression (a glance in his or her direction, raising the eyebrows expectantly).
- In the absence of a response by the child, rephrasing of questions that gives hints about how to respond, moving from open-ended questions to those that offer a structured choice: "Where is the pirate going?" (no answer) "Is he going to look for the buried treasure or is he going to chase the other pirate boat?"
- Opportunities and invitations to use language in decontextualized settings – to talk about objects, events or experiences that are not part of the immediate environment: "What did you do at grandma's house?," "How did you make the pinwheel?," "What are you going to do when you go on vacation?," etc.
- Minimal use of directives ("Do this ...," "Don't do this ...," etc.).

I. FUNCTION

Goal: Understand and Use Nonverbal Features of Communication

LEVEL I	LEVEL II
EXAMPLE: rise in voice at the end of question, increase in volume, accent on word(s) to indicate urgency, etc.	
• Adapt the volume of his or her voice to different settings and for different purposes: inside/outside, classroom/playground, restaurant/theater, dialogue/conversation, attracting attention, etc.	• Understand and use intonation and emphasis to ask a question, express surprise, agreement, displeasure, urgency.

Goal: Understand and Use Language to Communicate

LEVEL I	LEVEL II
CONVERSING:	CONVERSING:

NOTE: The key difference between Level I and II competencies in conversing is that at Level I an adult partner might lead or encourage conversation. At Level II, in order to converse with a peer, the child must be able to do so in-dependently, without prompting.

• Carry on a dialogue or conversation, initiating comments or responding to a partner's comments, with an adult.

• Carry on a dialogue or conversation, initiating comments or responding to a partner's comments, with another child of approximately the same age.

EXAMPLE: "Hello," pause for response by the caller, followed by an appropriate comment – "Just a minute," "I'll get my Mom," etc.

• Answer the telephone appropriately.

• Carry on a simple conversation on the telephone.

ASSERTING STATE OF BEING, NEEDS, AND DESIRES:

ASSERTING STATE OF BEING, NEEDS, AND DESIRES:

EXAMPLE: I have to go to the bathroom. I want to ride the bike.

• Express personal needs and desires verbally in a comprehensible manner.

EXAMPLE: ache, afraid, angry, cold, disappointed, don't understand, eager, excited, frustrated, full, happy, hot, hungry, hurt, impatient, interested, looking forward to, mad, pain, sad, satisfied, sick, sleepy, sore, surprised, thirsty, understand, worried.

• Identify and express physical sensations, mental states and emotional feelings, using words.

Goal: Understand and Use Language to Communicate, continued

LEVEL I	LEVEL II
NARRATING:	NARRATING:

- Given a picture, individual object or person within view:

  - indicate the picture or object, amongst several choices, that has been described.

  - describe its attributes so that someone else may identify it.

NOTE: The child may draw his own pictures, may use stickers, flannel board pictures, and so on to recreate a scene.

- Given an oral description of a scene, recreate the scene using pictures.

- Describe oneself, home and the immediate members of family (names, role in family, physical description, job/activities during the day, etc.)

- Sequence and describe images of events or phases of a single event that have been experienced:

EXAMPLE: getting dressed, going to the park, eating dinner, etc.

  - 3 images/events, occurring at temporally distinct times of the day.

EXAMPLE: steps in brushing teeth, making a cake, etc.

- Sequence and describe images of events or phases of a single event that have been experienced:

  - 3-5 images/events or phases of an event.

- Describe an event or task that:

EXAMPLE: play activities, such as coloring a picture, building with blocks, etc.

  - he or she is in the process of completing.

EXAMPLE: eating lunch, going to the store, etc.

  - he or she has just experienced, in the immediate past.

- Describe an event or personal experience that:

EXAMPLE: something that happened the day before, etc.

EXAMPLE: an upcoming vacation, plans for a birthday party, etc.

  - has taken place outside of the immediate time and place.

  - will take place.

Goal: Understand and Use Language to Communicate, continued

|

EXPLAINING/DIRECTING:

EXAMPLE: Turn off the light.

- Give simple directions: single-step directions.

EXAMPLE: Please give me a cookie and then read me a story.

- Give simple directions: multi-step directions.

NOTE: The teacher may first provide a demonstration of how to do something so that the child may then use words to explain the same directions to someone else.

- Give a sufficiently detailed and sequential explanation of how to do something (play a simple game, make a simple craft or recipe, etc.) so that the activity can be correctly carried out by another person.

EXPRESSING A POINT OF VIEW AND IMAGINING:

EXAMPLE: I like chocolate ice cream better than vanilla. I think we should go swimming instead of going to the playground because it's hot outside.

- Express a personal opinion.

EXAMPLE: (If I were the dragon in the story), I'd scare everyone away by breathing hot fire. (If I were a farmer), I'd get up early each morning to feed the animals. (If I were Timmy), I'd be angry that John took the blocks I was using.

- Assume a different role or perspective and express different possibilities, either imaginary or realistic.

Goal: Understand and Use Language to Think:
Organize, Relate and Analyze Information

LEVEL I	LEVEL II
PREDICTING:	**PREDICTING:**

EXAMPLE What will happen if we go outside without our coats? ...What if it starts to rain?

- Answer "what will happen if..." questions.

EXAMPLE: The ice cubes melted because we forgot to put the tray back in the freezer.

- Identify outcomes (what happened) and possible causes.

RELATING CONCEPTS AND REASONING LOGICALLY:	RELATING CONCEPTS AND REASONING LOGICALLY:

- Match pictures of simple opposites: big-little; cold-hot; dry-wet; full-empty; happy-sad; open-close.

- Identify and name simple opposites: big-little; large-small; cold-hot; loud-quiet; dry-wet; on-off; fast-slow; open-close; full-empty; rough-smooth; happy-sad; tall-short; hard-soft; up-down; yes-no.

EXAMPLE: food: apple, ice cream, cookie, hamburger, etc.; **clothing:** jacket, sock, shirt, dress, etc.; **toys:** ball, doll, blocks, puzzle, etc.; **household items:** refrigerator, bed, table, sofa, etc.; **people:** man, woman, girl, policeman, etc.; **animals:** cat, dog, horse, lion, etc.; **transportation:** car, truck, plane, train, etc.

- Sort, classify and describe objects and pictures, according to conceptual categories. (See sorting and classification competencies listed under Mathematical Reasoning and Number Sense.)

II. FORM

<u>NOTE:</u>
The vocabulary words included below are a representative, not comprehensive, listing.

Vocabulary words included within the context of an actual goal are those specific words presented in other sections of the Preschool Sequence, Mathematical Reasoning and Number Sense, Orientation in Space, and so on. When part of the goal, the intent is that pre-school children will understand and use these specific words in their own speech.

In most instances, however, specific vocabulary words are not included as part of a goal. Instead, a list of words is presented under the "Examples/Notes" heading as but one illustration of how different words may be used to convey nuances in meaning. Innumerable experiences, and thus possible word choices, will arise throughout the day. Teachers are encouraged to consciously respond to children's language by introducing vocabulary with increasingly subtle and precise meaning, as illustrated by the examples.

(In the following lists, some words are presented as hyphenated pairs to indicate that there is a logical relationship between the words; it may be helpful to provide experiences that allow the child to compare and contrast these particular words.)

Goal: Understand and Use Increasingly Varied and Complex Vocabulary and Syntax

LEVEL I	LEVEL II
• Use increasingly precise vocabulary in describing his immediate environment at home, in the neighborhood, at school, etc.	• Use increasingly precise vocabulary in describing his immediate environment at home, in the neighborhood, at school, etc.
• nouns/word labels within the following general categories: body parts, food, clothing, toys, household items, people (family, community helpers), animals, transportation, environment, etc.	• nouns/word labels within the following general categories: body parts, food, clothing, toys, household items, people (family, community helpers), animals, transportation, environment, etc.

EXAMPLE: **food:** bread, biscuit, muffin, roll, slice, etc.; **clothing:** coat, jacket, sweater, sweatshirt, vest, etc.; **toys:** bike, tricycle, dominoes game, lotto, etc.; **household items:** cup, glass, mug, etc.; **people:** daughter, female, girl, grandmother, mother, sister, woman, etc.; **animals:** cat, kitten, lion, tiger, etc.; **transportation:** automobile, car, taxi, etc.; **environment:** pond, puddle, etc. (See Orientation in Space)

NOTE: See Autonomy and Social Skills for goals relating to body image.

VOCABULARY

VOCABULARY	VOCABULARY
• body parts: ankle, arm, back, body, cheek, chest, chin, ear, elbow, eyebrow, eyelash, face, finger, foot, forehead, hair, hand, head, heel, hip, knee, lips, mouth, nail, neck, nose, shoulder, stomach, teeth, toe, tongue, waist, wrist	• body parts: ankle, arm, back, body, cheek, chest, chin, ear, elbow, eyebrow, eyelash, face, finger, foot, forehead, hair, hand, head, heel, hip, knee, lips, mouth, nail, neck, nose, shoulder, stomach, teeth, toe, tongue, waist, wrist

Goal: Understand and Use Increasingly Varied and Complex Vocabulary and Syntax, continued

	LEVEL I	LEVEL II
EXAMPLE: talk: speak, shout, whisper, etc.; **cut:** chop, saw, slice, snip, etc.	• verbs/action words.	• verbs/action words.
	• adjectives/describing words: color, size, shape, quantity and attributes based on the other senses.	• adjectives/describing words: color, size, shape, quantity and attributes based on the other senses.
	VOCABULARY	**VOCABULARY**
NOTE: See Visual Arts.	• **color:** black, blue, brown, green, orange, purple, red, white, yellow.	
NOTE: See Mathematical Reasoning and Number Sense	• **shape:** circle.	• **shape:** circle, rectangle, triangle.
NOTE: See Mathematical Reasoning and Number Sense		• **size:** large-small; wide-narrow; big-little; full-empty; tall-short; heavy-light; long-short; thick-thin.
NOTE: See Mathematical Reasoning and Number Sense	• **quantity:** any-some; all-none; more-less; most-least; many-few; equal; number words (one-four).	• **quantity:** any-some; all-none; more-less; most-least; many-few; equal; number words (one-ten).
NOTE: See Scientific Reasoning and the Physical World.	• **attributes based on other senses:** sweet-sour-salty; loud-quiet; hard-soft; rough-smooth; flexible-stiff; hot-cold; wet-dry.	
EXAMPLE: beautiful, dirty, fat, furry, gigantic, silly, tiny, ugly, etc.		• other adjectives.
EXAMPLE: better, easily, happily, loudly, quickly, quietly, slowly, too much, well, etc.		• adverbs/describing words.

Goal: Understand and Use Increasingly Varied and Complex Vocabulary and Syntax, continued

LEVEL I	LEVEL II
• **words indicating time:**	• **words indicating time:**

EXAMPLE: See Orientation in Time.

LEVEL I

VOCABULARY

- today-tomorrow; before-after; now; first-last; day-morning-afternoon-evening-night; name of current day; week; weekend; once upon a time; finally.

LEVEL II

VOCABULARY

- today-tomorrow-yesterday; always-never-sometimes; before-after; now-immediately-in a little while; first-last; beginning-middle-end; then-next; already; soon; during-while; later; day-morning-afternoon-evening-night; names of days (in sequence); month; season; names of the seasons (spring, summer...); week; weekend; year; once upon a time; finally.

EXAMPLE: See Orientation in Space.

LEVEL I

• **words indicating space:**

VOCABULARY

- there-here; in-on; in front of-behind; at the top of-at the bottom of; under; next to-in the middle of; near-far; around; to the side; in a line/row; in a circle; up-down.

LEVEL II

• **words indicating space:**

VOCABULARY

- there-here; in-on; in front of-behind; at the top of-at the bottom of; under-over, above-below; next to-in the middle of; near-far; inside-outside; around-between; at the corner of; against-toward-away; to the side; in a line/row; in a circle; up-down; high-low; left-right; front-back; face to face-back to back; before-after.

EXAMPLE: I am playing, I played; I am eating, I ate; he has, he had; you are, you were, etc.

LEVEL I

• Use different verb tenses: present and past tense.

EXAMPLE: I will play; I will eat, I am going to eat; she will have; we will be, etc.

LEVEL II

• Use different verb tenses: future tense.

NOTE: Elaborated sentences expand upon a simple "subject-verb" construction, such as, The girl is eating, by including the increased use of adjectives and adverbs, direct and indirect objects, such as, The (hungry little) girl is (slowly) eating (a big, red, apple).

LEVEL I

• Understand and use increasingly detailed elaborated declarative sentences.

Oral Language

Goal: Understand and Use Increasingly Varied and Complex Vocabulary and Syntax, continued

LEVEL I	LEVEL II

EXAMPLE: **ask questions:** Who ate the chocolate cookie? What game do you want to play? Where did you put my coat? When will we go swimming? Why did you open the window? **answer questions:** (who - person/character): Sam or Sam ate the chocolate cookie; (what - thing): Candyland or I want to play Candyland; (where -place): in the closet or I put your coat in the closet; (why - reason): because it's hot or I opened the window because it's hot.

- Ask or answer questions beginning with who, what, where, when, why.

NOTE: Elaborated questions expand upon a simple subject-verb construction, such as, Is the girl eating?, by including the increased use of adjectives and adverbs, direct and indirect objects, such as, Is the (little) girl (slowly) eating (a big, red apple)?

- Ask or answer increasingly detailed, elaborated questions (other than those beginning with who, what ,where, when, why).

NOTE: Elaborated imperatives expand upon a simple, one word command, such as Run!, by including the increased use of adverbs, prepositional phrases, such as Run (quickly) (to the tree)!

- Understand and use increasingly detailed, elaborated imperatives.

EXAMPLE: The (little) girl is not eating (a big, red apple). Isn't the (little) girl eating (a big, red apple)? Don't run (quickly)!

- Understand and use the negative forms of declarative sentences, questions and imperatives.

EXAMPLE: My brother has a dog and cat.

- Combine simple sentences using "and."

EXAMPLE: My toy truck has a horn, but it doesn't have lights. You may have cake or ice cream.

- Combine simple sentences using "but," "or."

Goal: Understand and Use Increasingly Varied and Complex Vocabulary and Syntax, continued

LEVEL I	LEVEL II

EXAMPLE: I want to play ball.

- Use personal pronouns correctly, especially "I," when referring to oneself.

EXAMPLE: My bathing suit is wet because I went swimming; If it snows tonight, we will build a snowman tomorrow; As soon as Dad comes home from work, we will go to the park; Please turn on the water in the bath tub, so that you can take a bath; Mother prepared the frosting while the cake was baking; He got dressed before he ate breakfast; You can have dessert after you eat your dinner; The man who fixed our car was very nice; The bike that I liked is red and blue; I will read you a story when you get in bed; I got my feet wet jumping in the puddles.

- Understand and use complex sentences with clauses introduced by the following words: because, if, as soon as, so that, while, before, after, who, that, when, (verb) + ing.

Language of Instruction

TEACHER AND CHILDREN	TEACHER ONLY	
	category	quiet
	conversation	talk
	describe	whisper
	directions	yell
	explain	
	group	
	in order	
	loud	
	opposite	
	question	

NOTE: Specific vocabulary for Teacher and Children is listed separately within other sections of the Preschool Sequence, such as Autonomy and Social Skills, Work Habits, Mathematical Reasoning and Number Sense, Orientation in Space, and so on.

NOTE: For a full discussion, please see "Language of Instruction," in the Preschool Sequence Introduction and in the Implementation section.

EXAMPLE: Use vocabulary from the Oral Language section as follows:

ADULT: Here are some pictures of different things. See – here's a picture of an apple, an ice cream cone, a dress, a cookie, a pair of shoes, a jacket, a pair of pants and a hamburger. Some of these pictures " go together." They belong to the same *group* of things; they belong to the same *category*. See – I can put the apple, the ice cream cone and the cookie all together in a *group*: they are all things that we can eat; they belong to the food *category*. Do you see another picture that belongs to the food *category*?

CHILD: (points to the picture of the hamburger)

ADULT: That's right – we can eat an apple, ice cream cone, cookie or a ....? (points to picture of hamburger and pauses expectantly)

CHILD: Hamburger.

ADULT: (nods) ...So they all belong to the food *category*. Here are some other pictures that belong to another *group* or *category*.

Nursery
Rhymes,
Poems,
Fingerplays,
and Songs

Nursery Rhymes, Poems, Fingerplays and Songs

OVERVIEW: The goals in this section introduce young children to nursery rhymes, poems, fingerplays, and songs— listening to and keeping the beat, listening to and interpreting the simple words of a given selection with gestures and actions, as well as learning about rhyming words. In addition to the sheer enjoyment of listening to and repeating the rhythmic and musical combination of words, learning these selections provides skill and discipline in developing the ability to memorize and further extends children's understanding and use of both the form and function of language.

By listening to and reciting these poems and songs, children have an opportunity to model and practice various oral language skills, including pronunciation, vocabulary and syntax. They can then build upon their familiarity with certain well known rhymes by experimenting with rhyming words. This competency, in turn, focuses attention on the sounds of language, a skill that will enhance later efforts in initial reading.

In addition to providing experiences with the form of language, these selections introduce children to hearing more formal written language. The language of the "little stories" of these poems and songs differs from the contextualized language of daily conversations. Their brevity makes them an ideal transition to the narrative language of storybooks.

Goal: Develop Memorization Skills

LEVEL I	LEVEL II
• Memorize and recite with others a simple nursery rhyme, poem or song.	• Memorize and recite independently a simple nursery rhyme, poem or song.

Goal: Listen to Nursery Rhymes, Poems, Fingerplays and Songs and Respond with Appropriate Gestures

LEVEL I	LEVEL II
• While listening to the recitation of a familiar nursery rhyme, poem or fingerplay, clap or tap the beat with hands and/or feet.	
• While listening to the recitation of a familiar nursery rhyme, poem or fingerplay, perform the associated hand and body gestures that have been previously taught.	
	• Interpret and act out through pantomime a nursery rhyme, poem or fingerplay, using one's own gestures and movements (as compared to those which have been previously demonstrated and taught).

Goal: Develop a Sense of Rhyme

LEVEL I	LEVEL II

EXAMPLE: Higglety, pigglety, pop!
The dog has eaten the ...(mop). The
pig's in a hurry, The cat's in a
...(flurry), Higglety, pigglety, pop!

• Using familiar rhymes, poems or songs, finish a recitation that has been begun with the correct rhyming word.

EXAMPLE: Higglety, pigglety, pop!
The dog has eaten the ...(top, crop, hop, zop). The pig's in a hurry, The cat's in a ...(scurry, blurry, furry), Higglety, pigglety, pop!

• Using familiar rhymes, poems or songs, indicate several possible rhyming word choices, other than those contained in the actual rhyme, to finish the recitation (nonsense words are acceptable).

Mother Goose and Other Traditional Rhymes:
The rhymes noted below represent a core selection for young children. They will delight in listening to the strong rhythm and rhyme, and sometimes, the sheer nonsense, of these selections. With repeated exposure, they will take pleasure in learning some of their favorites by heart.

A Hunting We Will Go
Bat, Bat
Bobby Shafto
Diddle, Diddle Dumpling, My Son John (K)
Doctor Foster
Here We Go Round the Mulberry Bush
Hickety, Pickety, My Black Hen
Lucy Locket
Once I Saw a Little Bird
One for the Money
One Misty, Moisty Morning
Pat-a-Cake (K)
Pease Porridge Hot
Peter, Peter Pumpkin Eater
Polly Put the Kettle On
Pussy Cat, Pussy Cat
Rain, Rain Go Away (K)
Ride a Cock Horse
Ring Around the Rosey (K)
Rock-a-bye, Baby (K)
The Old Woman Must Stand at the Tub, Tub, Tub
There was a Crooked Man
This Is the Way the Ladies Ride
This Little Piggy Went to Market (K)
To Market, To Market
Tom, Tom, the Piper's Son
Two Little Blackbirds
Wee Willie Winkie

Other Poems:

In addition to the Mother Goose rhymes listed above, young children should have many other opportunities to listen to poetry, old and new. They will enjoy the playful use of language in most poetry, the cadence and the frequent use of rhyming words. Read poems aloud, encouraging children's participation. The selected poems particularly lend themselves to pantomime and/or rhyming activities:

An Old Person From Ware (Edward Lear)
At the Seaside (Robert Louis Stevenson)
Higglety, Pigglety, Pop! (Samuel Goodrich)
Jack-o-Lantern (Aileen Fisher)
January (Maurice Sendak)
Jump or Jiggle (Evelyn Beyer)
Raindrops (Aileen Fischer)
Singing Time (Rose Fyleman)
The Pancake (Christine Rossetti)
The Worm (Ralph Bergengren)
There Was a Fat Pig (Arnold Lobel)

Fingerplays and Songs:

The following titles represent a core of traditional songs and fingerplays for young children. They will enjoy listening to and singing these selections. Teachers and parents are encouraged to supplement these recommendations with additional selections from popular, contemporary children's music.

A Tisket, A Tasket
Are You Sleeping?
Bingo (K)
Blue-Tail Fly (Jimmie Crack Corn)
Do Your Ears Hang Low?
Did You Ever See a Lassie?
Eensy, Weensy Spider
Five Little Ducks That I Once Knew
Five Little Monkeys Jumping On the Bed
Happy Birthday to You
Head and Shoulder, Knees and Toes
Here is the Beehive
Hush Little Baby (K)
I Know an Old Lady
If You're Happy and You Know It (K)
I'm a Little Teapot
John Jacob Jingleheimer Schmidt
Kookaburra
Lazy Mary
Looby Loo
Oats, Peas, Beans and Barley Grow
Oh, Dear What Can the Matter Be? (1)
Oh, Do You Know the Muffin Man?
Oh Where, Oh Where, Has My Little Dog Gone?
Old MacDonald (K)
One Potato, Two Potato
Open, Shut Them
Pop Goes the Weasel
Row, Row, Row Your Boat (1)
Teddy Bear, Teddy Bear, Turn Around
Teddy Bears' Picnic
Twinkle, Twinkle Little Star (K)
The Wheels on the Bus (K)
Where is Thumbkin?

Fingerplays and Songs, continued:
Who Stole the Cookie from the Cookie Jar?
Yankee Doodle (1)
You Are My Sunshine

Other:
Pledge of Allegiance

Language of Instruction

TEACHER AND CHILDREN		TEACHER ONLY	
		author	refrain
		beat	repeat
		clap	rhyme
		echo	rhyming word
		fingerplay	song
		pantomime	tap
		poem	title
		recite	verse

NOTE: For a full discussion, please see "Language of Instruction," in the Preschool Sequence Introduction and in the Implementation section.

EXAMPLE: Use vocabulary from the Nursery Rhymes, Poems, Fingerplays and Songs section as follows:

ADULT: Listen to this nursery *rhyme* while I *recite* it – it has *rhyming words:*
To market, to market, to buy a fat pig (emphasis on pig)
Home again, home again, jiggety-jig. (emphasis on jig).
Pig and jig are *rhyming words* – pig-jig; they have the same ending sound.

Listen again for the *rhyming words* and try to say or *echo* the *rhyming words* with me:
To market, to market, to buy a fat (pause – child and adult together): p...ig
Home again, home again, jiggety (pause – child and adult together): j...ig.

Did you hear the two *rhyming words?* pig and ...

CHILD: jig.

ADULT: That's right – pig and jig are *rhyming words.* Now listen while I *recite* another *verse* – there are some other *rhyming words.*
To market, to market, to buy a fat hog (emphasis on hog)
Home again, home again, jiggety-jog (emphasis on jog), etc.

Storybook Reading and Storytelling
6

Storybook Reading and Storytelling

OVERVIEW: The goals of this section focus on the language skills that children acquire when given the opportunity to hear the language of storybooks. In listening to and talking about stories that are read aloud, children build both listening and speaking skills. They are introduced to new vocabulary and formal written syntax, ways of linking and relating ideas. They also refine skills in:

- Narrating: understanding and describing illustrations, understanding and describing the setting, characters and events of stories and so on
- Predicting: telling what will happen next in a story or suggesting a possible alternative ending
- Imagining: telling their own stories, either based on illustrations or creating a story using their imagination.

In addition, early experiences with books also lay the foundation for concepts and skills that children will later use as they begin to read and write. They learn about book format – the arrangement of covers, pages, individual printed words and letters – and they gain insight into the elements of a story – setting, characters, the pursuit of a goal or the resolution of a problem in a sequential series of events – an understanding that is instrumental for reading comprehension.

Goal: Listen to Stories Read Aloud

LEVEL I	LEVEL II
NARRATING	NARRATING
• Attend and listen to illustrated picture books with simple story lines during a 15 minute reading.	• Attend and listen to picture books with storylines (30 minutes), as well as books of other genres, such as informational books (15 minutes).
• Hold a book correctly, turning the pages in accordance with the story being read aloud, from beginning to end.	• Attend and listen to books with minimal or no illustrations during a 15 minute reading.
• Find the object within an illustration or find the illustration within the book that is being described.	
• Answer questions about the elements of a story: character(s), setting, plot and events.	

NOTE: The 15 and 30 minute time references are intended to be end-of-the-year goals for children actively engaged in listening to a story in a small or large group setting.

Goal: Participate in Stories Read Aloud

LEVEL I	LEVEL II
NARRATING	**NARRATING**

- Describe an illustration.

- In books with repetitive phrases or a refrain, provide or join in repeating the refrain aloud.

Goal: Develop a Notion of "Story Schema"

LEVEL I	LEVEL II
NARRATING	**NARRATING**

NOTE: Beginning practice in retelling a story may take many forms in addition to verbally recounting the story. Children may retell a story by referring to and sequentially describing story illustrations, acting out the story, telling the story with puppets or flannel board figures, and so on.

LEVEL I — NARRATING

- Retell a story that has been read aloud; include character(s), a beginning, the plot (central idea) of the story, and an ending.

- Sequence 3 illustrations of events from a story.

LEVEL II — NARRATING

- Retell a story that has been read aloud; include character(s), setting (time, place), the plot (central idea) of the story, the sequential events and an ending.

- Sequence 5 illustrations of events from a story.

PREDICTING

- Predict events in a story, i.e., what will happen next?

- Provide a story ending consistent with other given story events.

LEVEL I — EXPRESSING A POINT OF VIEW/IMAGINING

- "Read"/tell a story using a wordless picture book.

LEVEL II — EXPRESSING A POINT OF VIEW/IMAGINING

- "Read"/tell a story based on the illustrations of a book with text that has not been read aloud previously.

- Make up and tell a story.

Goal: Demonstrate an Awareness of Book and Print (Written Language) Organization

LEVEL I	LEVEL II
• Identify previously read books by title and cover.	• Point to: the title of a book; the top, bottom or middle of a page; the beginning of the book (first page); where to start reading a book (first word on the first page); the order that words are read on a page (left to right, line to line); the end of the book (last page); a word; a letter.
	• Using cover and illustration cues, locate those books in a collection of books that pertain to a general topic or might answer a question.
	• Point to words that begin with the same letter as own name.

NOTE:

The titles listed below constitute a core of traditional stories and tales for young children.

Stories:

Goldilocks and the Three Bears (K)
The Gingerbread Boy
How Turtle Flew South for the Winter (or, Why Turtle Has a Cracked Shell)
(Native American: Dakota Legend)
The Little Red Hen (K)
The Shoemaker and the Elves (Brothers Grimm)
The Three Little Pigs (K)
Thumbelina (Hans Christian Anderson)
Why Flies Buzz (African folktale)

Aesop's Fables:

The Lion and the Mouse (K)
The Town Mouse and the Country Mouse

Legends and Stories of America's Past:

Thanksgiving Day celebration between the Indians and the Pilgrims (K)
George Washington and the cherry tree(K)
Betsy Ross and the flag (1)
Abraham Lincoln and his humble origins(K)
Martin Luther King (2)

Books:

In addition to the traditional stories and tales listed above, young children should be exposed to many more stories, including classic picture books, read-aloud books, "Dr. Seuss" books and other perennial favorites. ABC books, wordless picture books to encourage storytelling and simple chapter books with limited illustrations are valuable additions as well. Some suggested titles are listed below. Young children should also have an opportunity to hear non-fiction books read aloud – books on art and music, books which describe the world around them – animals, plants, different places and people, and so on.

Some Suggested Storybooks:

A Boy, A Dog, A Frog – M. Mayer (Dial, 1985)
Amazing Grace – M. Hoffman (Dial, 1991)
Are You My Mother? – P.D.Eastman (Random House, 1960)
Ask Mr. Bear – M. Flack (Macmillan, 1968)
Blueberries for Sal – R. McCloskey (Puffin, 1976)
Bobo's Magic Wishes – J. Palazzo-Craig (Troll, 1996)
Brown Bear, Brown Bear, What Do You See? – B. Martin
(Holt, Rinehart, & Winston, 1992)
Caps for Sale – Slobodkina (Harper Collins, 1987)
The Carrot Seed – R. Krauss (Harper Collins, 1989)
Cat in the Hat – Dr. Seuss (Random House, 1957)
Chicka Chicka Boom Boom – B. Martin & J. Archambault (Simon & Schuster, 1989)
Corduroy – D. Freeman (Puffin, 1993)
Curious George – H.A.Rey (Houghton Mifflin, 1941)
Frederick – L. Lionni (Knopf, 1973)
Good Dog, Carl – A. Day (Simon & Schuster, 1997)
Goodnight Gorilla – P. Rathmann (Penguin Putnam, 1994)
Harold and the Purple Crayon – C. Johnson (Harper Collins, 1981)
I Know an Old Lady Who Swallowed a Fly – C. & J. Hawkins (Putnam, 1987)
The Little Engine That Could – W. Piper (Putnam, 1990)
The Littles – J. Peterson (Scholastic, 1993)
Madeline – L. Bemmelmans (Puffin, 1993)
Make Way for Ducklings – R. McCloskey (Puffin, 1976)
Mike Mulligan and His Steam Shovel – V. Burton (Houghton Mifflin, 1977)
Millions of Cats – W. Gag (Putnam, 1977)
Miss Rumphius – B. Cooney (Puffin, 1985)
Mufaro's Beautiful Daughters – J. Steptoe (Scholastic, 1987)
My Father's Dragon – R. Gannett (Knopf, 1987)
The Park Bench – F. Takeshita (Kane/Miller, 1989)
The Red Balloon – A. Lamourisse (Doubleday, 1977)
The Runaway Bunny – M. Wise (Harper & Row, 1977)
Sam and the Tigers – J. Lester (Dial, 1996)
The Snowy Day – E. Keats (Puffin, 1976)
The Story of Ferdinand – M. Leaf (Puffin, 1993)
Strega Nona – T. DePaola (Simon & Schuster, 1979))
Swimmy – L. Lionni (Knopf, 1987)
The Tale of Rabbit & Coyote – T. Johnson (Putnam & Grosset, 1994)
Tikki Tikki Tembo – A. Mosel (Scholastic, 1968)
The Very Hungry Caterpillar – E. Carle (Putnam, 1981)
Uncle Jed's Barbershop – M Mitchell (Simon & Schuster, 1993)
Where the Wild Things Are – M. Sendak (Harper Collins, 1968)

Non-Fiction Books:

A Child's Book of Art – Great Pictures, Great Words – L. Micklethwait (Dorling Kindersley, 1993) as well as the "I Spy" and "Spot A..." books by the same author.
Children Just Like Me – S. Copsey, et.al. (Dorling Kindersley, 1995)
Eye Openers Series and *Eyewitness Juniors Series* (Dorling Kindersley) [a series of colorful books on various animals]
First Discovery Series (Scholastic) [a series of colorful, informative books, with plastic overlays; some titles – *Fruits, Vegetables, Flowers, Trees, The Seashore, Whales, Under the Ground, The Egg, Colors, Light*]
People – P. Spier (Doubleday, 1988)
Picture Dictionary

Language of Instruction

NOTE: For a full discussion, please see "Language of Instruction," in the Preschool Sequence Introduction and in the Implementation section.

TEACHER & CHILDREN	TEACHER ONLY	
after	at last	page
bottom	author	read
end	beginning	refrain
first	character	retell
finally	cover	title
middle	events	write
next	illustration	word
once upon a time	illustrator	
top	in order	
then	letter	

EXAMPLE: Use vocabulary from the Storybook Reading and Storytelling section as follows:

ADULT: Do you remember yesterday that we *read* the story, *The Red Balloon*? Today, we are going to look at the *illustrations* in *The Red Balloon*, the pictures. I want you to *retell* the story of *The Red Balloon*. We'll look at each *illustration in order* and you'll tell me what was happening in the story. Here's the *first illustration* – tell me about the *characters* – who you see in the picture – and what was happening.

CHILD: This is Pascal and, etc.

Emerging Literacy Skills in Reading and Writing

7

Emerging Literacy Skills in Reading and Writing

OVERVIEW: This section builds on the language skills described in the preceding sections. The competencies described here go beyond oral language skills to early reading and writing skills. The goals ask children to add to their prior experiences with printed words in books by recognizing print in the daily environment and some ways it is used: to identify, to name or label (food, toys, streets, stores, etc.), to make lists, report events, give directions, communicate messages, and more.

The section focuses on the relation between oral language and print. The goals ask children to associate specific familiar spoken words, such as their own names or names of familiar objects, with specific written words. Children then go on to recognize that the distinct marks that make up each word are the letters in our alphabet. Children learn that these letters have names through such means as singing the alphabet song. They learn to identify and name the specific letters in their own names.

A crucial part of learning to read is developing phonemic awareness, the understanding that individual sounds are associated with individual letters and combinations of letters. To help children begin to develop phonemic awareness, the goals in this section ask children not only to refine their visual recognition of print but also to attend to the spoken sounds of language (for related topics, see the clapping and rhyming skills described in Nursery Rhymes, Poems, Fingerplays and Songs). Children are asked to take apart and put together smaller and smaller units of sound, from individual words in a sentence, to syllables in words, to the beginning sounds in individual words.

The goals here also include the skills needed to produce print, that is, to write. At first, children are asked to perform manual activities that enhance both hand-eye coordination and small muscle control of the hand and fingers. They learn the proper way to hold a writing implement, as well as a variety of small designs and strokes that will eventually be combined to form letters. They are also asked to write their own names.

I. FUNCTION

Goal: Develop an Awareness of Written Matter/Print in Everyday Surroundings and Its Many Uses

LEVEL I	LEVEL II
• Identify different examples of print in the environment.	
NARRATING	**NARRATING**
• Collect objects using a list of words and pictures.	
• Dictate a caption for a drawing or photograph.	• Dictate a simple letter, invitation or thank you note.
• Use a simplified schedule of daily activities, depicted in pictures and words to describe the order of events for the day, i.e. which are the first and last activities.	• Use a simplified schedule of daily activities, depicted in words and pictures to indicate which activity preceded and which will follow the current activity.

EXAMPLE: in books, newspapers, magazines, on food containers, menus, mail, street signs, billboards, etc.

EXAMPLE: use a rebus and word list to go on a treasure or scavenger hunt.

EXAMPLE: photos of children engaged in daily activities (opening exercises, center time, snack time, etc.) arranged and listed in order on a bulletin board.

Goal: Develop an Awareness of Written Matter/Print in Everyday Surroundings and Its Many Uses, continued

LEVEL I	LEVEL II
NARRATING, continued:	**NARRATING, continued:**
	• Use a simplified telephone listing, depicted in words and pictures.
NARRATING OR IMAGINING:	**NARRATING OR IMAGINING:**
NOTE: A variety of methods may be used as "written expression," including the child's own drawings, other pictures, photos, rebuses, timelines, charts, invented spelling, etc.	• Depict and represent "in writing": people, objects, events or activities, derived from his or her own experience or imagination.
	• Dictate a description to accompany one's own drawings of people, objects, events or activities, based on his or her own experience or imagination.
DIRECTING/EXPLAINING:	**DIRECTING/EXPLAINING:**
NOTE: With adult supervision children should have the opportunity to actually carry out the recipe using real ingredients. They may also enjoy "pretend reenacting" the recipe afterwards.	• Follow a recipe depicted in words and pictures.
	• Assemble a simple object or craft following illustrated directions.
NOTE: See note above for example of possible written expression. NOTE: Examples of "scientific explanations" include observation and recording of animal or plant development, properties of air or light (See Scientific Reasoning and the Physical World).	• Depict "in writing": recipe or craft directions, scientific explanations of observed events or experiments.

II. FORM

Goal: Develop an Awareness of the Structure of Print

LEVEL I	LEVEL II
• Recognize the written form of his or her first name.	
• Recognize the initial letter of his or her first name.	
	• Sing the "Alphabet Song."
	• Read the first names of other family members or classmates.
	• Develop an understanding of the relationship between spoken and written language by associating written word units on word labels and signs with spoken words.
	• Isolate and point to individual words as distinct units on a page of print.
	• Make attempts at using invented (phonetic) spelling to communicate in writing.[1]

EXAMPLE: When presented with several upper case letters, the child should be able to point to which letter starts his or her name, although he or she may not yet be able to identify the letter by name.

NOTE: The goal in preschool is not to read or memorize flash cards of individual words, but to understand that a spoken word can be represented in writing. This association may be facilitated by attaching word labels to everyday objects in the classroom, and by helping children learn to recognize signs in the everyday environment ("Girls," "Boys," "Exit," "Stop," "Office," "Bus Stop," etc.)

NOTE: The goal is for the child to recognize how words are organized on a page, taking into account spacing within and between words.

[1]NOTE:

Regarding the use of invented spelling: Children use invented (phonetic) spelling when they attempt to write a word "the way they think it sounds." Preschool children should be encouraged to write on their own as this reinforces the understanding that ideas and spoken words can be represented on paper. As children become more aware of the role of letters and words, their writing evolves from random scribbles to efforts at writing individual letters, often writing a sequence of apparently unrelated individual letters to represent many words. The goal at this point is simply to reinforce the connection between spoken and written language, and the appreciation of how letters are used to communicate in writing. This appreciation will serve as a foundation for more systematic phonics and spelling instruction in associating specific sounds with specific letters in kindergarten and first grade.

Goal: **Develop Phonemic Awareness**

NOTE:
To further develop phonemic awareness, see also the Music section, especially "Listen to and Discriminate Differences in Sound" and "Imitate and Produce Sounds"; also see the Nursery Rhymes section, "Develop a Sense of Rhyme."

LEVEL I	LEVEL II
	• Segment a spoken sentence into separate, distinct words.
	• Blend spoken parts of a compound word and say a whole word, such as, "bill"-"board" – "billboard."
	• Blend two spoken syllables and say a whole word, such as, "pic"-"nic" = "picnic."
EXAMPLE: Which starts with "ssss" – soap or cup?	• Given a sound and a choice of two spoken words/pictures, identify the word that begins with the given sound.
NOTE: Child is to produce sound, not letter name.	• Given a spoken word/picture, give the beginning sound.
	• Indicate the number of phonemes (1-3) heard in a real or nonsense word by representing each phoneme heard with a token or object.
NOTE: Choose written letters from child's name for which there are 1-1 sound correlations, i.e., one letter makes one sound in the child's name.	• Develop an understanding of the relationship between written letters and spoken sounds, identifying by name all letters in his or her first name and also identifying the sound made by at least three letters in his or her first name. [1]

[1] NOTE:
Regarding letters and sounds: The intent is to establish [1] the general notion that written letters represent particular sounds and [2] that we can refer to letters by the sounds that they represent as well as by a name. These concepts are introduced using the child's own name, and they may be extended by providing children with many playful ways to explore words and language.

Given the opportunity, some children may go on to learn the names and sounds of other letters, as well. A balanced approach is recommended: while knowledge of the alphabet is essential in laying the foundation for initial reading, the other competencies and skills included in the *entire* Language section are also very important and should not be neglected in an attempt to teach "all the letters of the alphabet."

Goal: Develop the Fine Motor Skills and Strokes Used in Writing

LEVEL I	LEVEL II

EXAMPLE: using tweezers and eyedroppers, stringing beads, completing lacing pictures, putting pegs in pegboards, etc.

- Perform activities requiring small muscle control.

- Use hands, fingers, paintbrush, crayons, markers, pencil to produce written marks on both vertical and horizontal surfaces.

- Tear, fold, paste and glue paper.

- Given an outline of a simple shape or a line drawing of a large simple picture, color it, staying within the lines.

EXAMPLE: Mastery in copying and reproducing these individual writing strokes will enhance those specific fine motor skills that will be later used in writing the letters of the alphabet. It is recommended that the strokes be introduced in the order listed above. Many of the same strokes will be recombined to form the individual letters. Teachers are encouraged to incorporate practice of these strokes in creative art activities, rather than in repetitive rote practice.

- Draw on paper:

  - horizontal line ——
  - vertical line |
  - point •
  - circle ◯
  - spiral ◎

- Draw horizontal and vertical lines between two end points.

- Hold a writing instrument correctly between the thumb and index finger, resting against the middle finger.

EXAMPLE:

- Trace and then draw independently the outlines of geometric shapes (circle, triangle, rectangle) and irregular figures.

Goal: Develop the Fine Motor Skills and Strokes Used in Writing

LEVEL I	LEVEL II

EXAMPLE: Mastery in copying and reproducing these individual writing strokes will enhance those specific fine motor skills that children will use later in writing the letters of the alphabet. It is recommended that the strokes be introduced in the order listed above. Many of these same strokes will be recombined to form the individual letters. Teachers are encouraged to incorporate practice of these strokes in creative art activities, rather than in repetitive rote practice.

- [1]Draw on paper and use as motifs in designs:

  - horizontal line ⎯

  - vertical line |

  - point ·

  - diagonal line \ /

  - zigzag line \/\

  - circle ○

  - spiral ◎

  - moon ⊂

  - cross †

  - cane ↄ

  - hook ∪

  - bowl ∪

  - bridge ∩

  - wave ∽∽∽

  - x ✕

  - star ✳

EXAMPLE: Variations in letter size and orientation, spacing, etc., are characteristic of preschool writing. The focus is on sufficient legibility so that the written name can generally be recognized by other children and adults. Children should be taught to write the first letter of their name as an uppercase letter and the remaining letters as lower case letters.

- Write his or her first name.

[1]**NOTE:**
For children in schools where "Denelian writing" is taught, add: single loop: _ℓ_ , connected loop: _ℓℓ_ .

Language of Instruction

TEACHER AND CHILDREN		TEACHER ONLY	
		SPECIFIC WRITING STROKES	MISCELLANEOUS
		bowl	ABCs
		bridge	alphabet
		cane	capital letter
		circle	color within the lines
		cross	connect the dots/points
		diagonal line	curved line
		hook	design
		horizontal line	dictate
		loop	directions
		moon	grid
		point	initial
		spiral	letter
		star	line
		vertical line	lower case letter
		wave	outline
		x	print
		zigzag line	read
			sound
			straight line
			title
			trace
			upper case letter
			word
			write

NOTE: For a full discussion, please see "Language of Instruction," in the Preschool Sequence Introduction and in the Implementation section.

NOTE:

For clarity in working and communicating with young children, some descriptive terms should be consistently used in describing the individual writing strokes listed on pages 58-59. The specific terms selected have no intrinsic value; the arbitrary names on pages 58-59 are but one possibility. Undue effort should not be expended in teaching these terms to young children as part of their speaking vocabulary. However, when formal writing instruction in letter formation begins (for example, when the child learns to write his own name), the same names may be used by the teacher in describing these strokes as the various component elements of individual letters.

EXAMPLE: Use vocabulary from the Emerging Literacy section as follows:

ADULT: I'm going to draw some *points*. Here are two *points*. I want you to *connect these points* with a *straight line*. Can you start at this *point* and, with your finger, show me how you would *connect these points* using a *straight line*?

CHILD: (traces line)

ADULT: Good. You made a *straight line* with your finger. ... Here's a piece of string. I'm going to hold one end of the string on one *point*. Can you use the rest of the string to make a *straight line* to *connect the two points*?

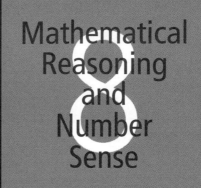

Mathematical
Reasoning
and
Number
Sense

8

Mathematical Reasoning and Number Sense

OVERVIEW: Young children seem to be naturally drawn to touching, manipulating, and examining the objects they find around them. The goals of this section build upon this curiosity and desire to explore. In the context of experiences with concrete objects and then with pictures, the child is asked to recognize similarities and differences, classify objects and shapes, recognize/create patterns in sequences of objects, and make comparisons among objects, using simple measurement skills. He or she is also asked to quantify small groups of objects, to count and to demonstrate a basic understanding of addition and subtraction as "putting together" and "taking away." In each instance, the child is asked to move from the concrete experience to representing knowledge symbolically using mathematical language, such as "more than," "less than," "longer," "shorter," number words ("three" and "four"), numerical symbols ("3" and "4"), and so on.

Goal: Sort and Classify Objects or Pictures of Objects

	LEVEL I	LEVEL II
EXAMPLE: block-ball, boat-house, circle-triangle.	• Identify pairs of objects or images as the "same" or "different," with "different" pairs varying in gross details.	
EXAMPLE: red ball-green ball, house with a chimney-house without a chimney, circle-oval.		• Identify pairs of objects or images as the "same" or "different," with "different" pairs increasingly similar, varying only in one or more minor detail(s) and with images becoming more abstract, symbolic.
	• Given a sample object/picture and verbal description of the selection criteria, sort objects/pictures according to a single criterion: (K)	
EXAMPLE: Find all that are red, like this one.	• **color:** red, yellow, green, blue, orange, purple, brown, black, white.	
EXAMPLE: Find all that are round (or a circle), like this one.	• **shape:** circle, triangle, rectangle.	
NOTE: In each sort, there will be only two categories, objects that possess the selection criteria and those that do not, i.e., "red" and "not red," "round" and "not round," etc.		

Goal: Sort and Classify Objects or Pictures of Objects, continued

LEVEL I	LEVEL II

LEVEL II

- Given a sample object/picture and verbal description of the selection criteria, sort objects/pictures according to a single criterion: (K)

  • **size:** small, medium, large; short, long.

  • **function**

EXAMPLE: Find all that are small, like this one.

EXAMPLE: Find all that you can wear, like this one.

NOTE: In each sort, there will be only two categories, objects that possess the selection criteria and those that do not, i.e., "small" and "not small," "can wear" and "cannot wear," etc.

LEVEL I

- Indicate whether an object belongs to a given collection.

NOTE: When classifying by a single criterion, there may be several categories. If the direction is to classify objects by color there may be a group of red objects, a group of yellow objects, a group of blue objects, etc.

- Classify objects/pictures using a single criterion: (K)
  • **color:** red, yellow, green, blue, orange, purple, brown, black, white.
  • **shape:** circle, triangle, rectangle.
  • **size:** small, medium, large; long, short.
  • **function**
  • **other conceptual categories:** animals, toys, clothing, attributes perceived by the five senses, etc.

EXAMPLE: They're all red.

- Identify and label verbally the single, common attribute or characteristic of a group of objects/pictures.

EXAMPLE: Everything in this group is red; in this one, yellow; and, in this one, green.

- Identify and label verbally the differences or criteria used for classification of several groups of objects/pictures.

EXAMPLE: Find the one that is blue and round.

- Select an object/picture, according to a description that includes two properties.

NOTE: Venn diagrams, in the form of manipulative, intersecting or nonintersecting circles (hula hoops) or paper and pencil representations, may be useful in visually depicting the sorting and classification of objects according to two properties.

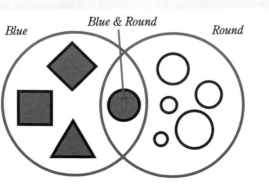

Blue   *Blue & Round*   *Round*

Goal: Sort and Classify Objects or Pictures of Objects, continued

LEVEL I	LEVEL II

NOTE: The terms "horizontal" and "vertical" are included for the teacher's reference only.

EXAMPLE: Complete the interior squares of a table having simple colors or designs along the horizontal axis and shapes, circle, rectangle and triangle, along the vertical axis.

• Use the criteria along the horizontal and vertical axes of a double-entry table to complete the interior squares of the table.

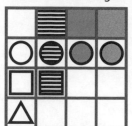

Goal: Duplicate and Continue Linear Patterns (K)

LEVEL I	LEVEL II

EXAMPLE: large red, round bead, large yellow, round bead, large red, round bead, large yellow, round bead, etc.

• Duplicate a pattern of 6-10 concrete objects in which one property (color, size or shape) is alternated.

• Match concrete objects arranged in a pattern (alternation of one attribute) with a corresponding drawing/pattern card.

• Using concrete objects, continue a given pattern of 5 objects (represented with concrete objects or by a pattern card drawing) in which one property is alternated (color, size or shape).

• Using concrete objects, continue a more complex two color pattern depicted by a pattern card: AABBAA... or BBABB... or AAABBAAABB..., etc.

EXAMPLE:

●■●○●■●○●

• Using stickers and/or colored markers, continue on paper either an alternating pattern of one property (color, size or shape) or a two color pattern.

EXAMPLE: The pattern is two red beads, one yellow bead, two red bead, one yellow bead...

• Create and verbally describe a pattern using concrete objects.

Goal: Perceive and Recognize Shapes

LEVEL I	LEVEL II

NOTE: For floor type puzzles with larger individual pieces, Level II criteria: at least 35 interlocking pieces.

• Complete 8½" x 11" (or larger) puzzles of at least 10 interlocking pieces.

• Complete 8½" x 11" (or larger) puzzles of at least 18 interlocking pieces.

• Match rectangular, square, circular, and triangular shapes to outlines of the same configuration and size.

• Given a collection of assorted shapes, sort and name the circles. (K)

• Given a collection of assorted shapes, classify and name circles, rectangles, and triangles. (K)

• Find examples of everyday objects in the shape of circles or rectangles. (K)

Goal: Use Simple Measurement Skills and Seriate Objects

LEVEL I	LEVEL II

LEVEL II

- Divide one item (cookie, candy bar, piece of paper, etc.) into approximately equal pieces for two people.

- Examine pairs of objects and use the following vocabulary to describe the objects: (K) (examine objects visually)

  - **length:** long-short

  - **height:** tall-short

  - **size:** large-small, thick-thin, wide-narrow

  - **volume:** full-empty

  - **mass:** heavy-light (examine by lifting objects)

  - **temperature:** hot-cold (examine by touch)

- Use an arbitrary tool of measurement (string, blocks, stick, hands, etc.) to compare the length and height of concrete objects and use the following comparative vocabulary:

  - **length:** longer-shorter

  - **height:** taller-shorter

NOTE: Child may mark measurement of each object directly on the ruler in order to make comparisons; reference to standard units of measure, such as inches, is not necessary.

- Use a straight edge or modified ruler to compare the length and height of concrete objects, using the following comparative vocabulary:

  - **length:** longer-shorter.

  - **height:** taller-shorter.

- Seriate at least 3 items by length, height or size, in ascending or descending order, and use the following comparative vocabulary:

  - **length:** longest-shortest.

  - **height:** tallest- shortest.

  - **size:** largest-smallest.

Goal: Quantify Groups of Objects

LEVEL I	LEVEL II
• Recite the number sequence: 1-4.	• Recite the number sequence: 1-10
• Compare two groups of concrete objects and use quantitative vocabulary to describe the groups (more than, less than, the same as) with up to 4 objects in each group. (K)	• Compare two groups of concrete objects and use quantitative vocabulary to describe the groups (more than, less than, the same as) with up to 6 objects in each group. (K)
• Demonstrate one-to-one correspondence with concrete objects, up to and including 4.	• Demonstrate one-to-one correspondence with concrete objects, up to and including 6.
• Construct a collection of objects so that it has the same number of objects as another collection, up to 4 items.	• Construct a collection of objects so that it has the same number of objects as a given numeral, up to 6.
• Count groups of concrete objects up to 4 objects in a group.	• Count groups of concrete objects up to 6 objects in a group.

EXAMPLE: as many place settings as dolls, paintbrushes as pots of paint, cookies as children, etc.

NOTE:

Traditionally, preschool programs have focused on teaching children to count objects up to 10. In the Preschool Sequence a conscious decision has been made to focus goals and experiences on developing in-depth understanding of quantitative concepts with a more limited number of objects.

This decision is based on cognitive learning research which reveals that, given the opportunity to explore the physical environment, very young children naturally acquire a global, quantitative appreciation of groups of objects. This natural awareness is limited, however, to quantities of up to four (4) objects.

Furthermore, this research also indicates that this natural awareness of limited quantities does not include the ability to represent or think about the quantities symbolically by using words, like more than, less than, one, two, or numerals, like 1, 2, to describe the quantities.

The goal then is to build upon these natural learnings by:
[1] firmly establishing the use of mathematical language and symbols to describe, compare and perform other mathematical operations.
[2] extend quantitative understanding to groups of objects beyond 4.

In the Preschool Sequence the goals focus on developing in-depth understanding of quantities of up to six (6) objects. This understanding will provide a solid foundation for then moving on to larger quantities.

Goal: Quantify Groups of Objects, continued

LEVEL I	LEVEL II

EXAMPLE: Make a group that has 4 blocks. Initially, the child should work with concrete, manipulative objects, i.e., blocks, beads, miniature toys. Once he or she consistently represents the correct quantity with manipulative objects, the transition should be made to a more abstract, representational level, i.e., using stickers on paper to represent the number of objects in a group, coloring the number of objects requested, etc.

• Given an oral number, create or represent a group with the correct number of objects, up to 4 objects in a group.

• Given an oral number, create or represent a group with the correct number of objects, up to 6 objects in a group.

• Name and match numerals 1-4 with corresponding quantities.

NOTE: Variations in number size and orientation, spacing, etc., are characteristic of preschool writing. The focus is on sufficient legibility such that the numerals can be read by other children and adults.

• Name and write numerals 1-6 with corresponding quantities.

• Arrange or write the numerals 1-6 in sequential order.

• Identify ordinal position for first and last.

• Play a simple game moving one's marker the number of spaces shown on a single die.

• Organize and read quantitative data in simple bar graphs.

Goal: Compare Written Numerals

LEVEL I	LEVEL II

EXAMPLE: Which is more, 3 or 2?

NOTE: When children first begin to work with written numerals, it is most important to facilitate the transition between the world of concrete, manipulative objects and the abstract symbols of numerals. Initially the written numerals should be paired and presented with manipulative objects. When children are asked to compare sets of numerals, their attention should be directed to both the objects and the numerals. Gradually, the concrete objects may be omitted, so that the comparison is made directly using only the written symbols, the numerals.

- Compare pairs of numerals 1-4 to determine more and less, or greater than/less than.

EXAMPLE: Which is more, 2 or 5?

- Compare pairs of numerals 1-6 to determine more and less, or greater than/less than.

Goal: Develop an Understanding of Addition and Subtraction

LEVEL I	LEVEL II

EXAMPLE: 1 object can be "put together" with 2 others to make a combined group of 3 objects.

- Illustrate the concept of "put together" and "take away" with groups of 1-4 objects (4 is the maximum number after adding or before subtracting): smaller quantities/groups can be "put together" to make larger quantities/groups; small quantities/groups can be "taken away" from large quantities/groups.

- Illustrate the concept of "put together" and "take away" with groups of 1-6 objects (6 is the maximum number after adding or before subtracting).

- Define "put together" as adding and "take away" as subtracting.

- Add and subtract using numerals 1-4 (4 is the maximum number after adding or before subtracting), using concrete objects or pictures as needed.

Goal: Identify Money

LEVEL I	LEVEL II
• Identify and count pennies, up to 4.	• Identify and count pennies, up to 6.
• Identify a one-dollar bill.	• Identify a quarter.
	• Indicate that a one-dollar bill has more value than one penny or quarter.

Language of Instruction

NOTE: For a full discussion, please see "Language of Instruction," in the Preschool Sequence Introduction and in the Implementation section.

TEACHER AND CHILDREN		TEACHER ONLY	
CLASSIFICATION	**MEASUREMENT AND SERIATION**	**CLASSIFICATION**	**MEASUREMENT AND SERIATION**
different	cold	classify	height
same	empty	color	in order
	first	property	length
QUANTITIES/COUNTING	full	sort	ruler
all	heavy	the same as	size
any	hot		
equal	last	**QUANTITIES/COUNTING**	**SHAPES**
fewer than	light	count	corner
larg(er) (est)	long(er) (est)	how many	cube
less than	middle	number	curved line
more than	narrow	compare	form
none	short(er) (est)		outline
small(er) (est)	tall(er) (est)	**MONEY**	pyramid
some	thick	bill	round
	thin	coin	shape
MONEY	wide	money	sphere
dollar			square
quarter		**ADDITION AND SUBTRACTION**	straight line
penny	**SHAPES**	add	
	circle	put together	**PATTERNS**
ADDITION AND SUBTRACTION	rectangle	subtract	pattern
	triangle	take away	continue the pattern
addition			extend the pattern
subtraction			
			MISCELLANEOUS
			math
			mathematics

EXAMPLE: Use vocabulary from the Mathematical Reasoning and Number Sense section as follows:

CHILD: Look – I made two piles.

ADULT: Let's see what you did. Ah, you *sorted* the beads into two *different* piles or groups. (Pointing) Is this group the *same* or *different* than this group?

CHILD: (no response).

ADULT: (Pointing) This group is d...

CHILD: ...*different*.

ADULT: This group is *different* from this group. Can you tell me how they are *different*?

CHILD: This has red things and this has blue things.

ADULT: Right – this group has red beads and this group has blue beads. You sorted the beads into two *different* groups according to their *color*. If I give you these other beads (pile of yellow and green beads), can you also *sort* them into two *different* groups according to their *color*?, etc.

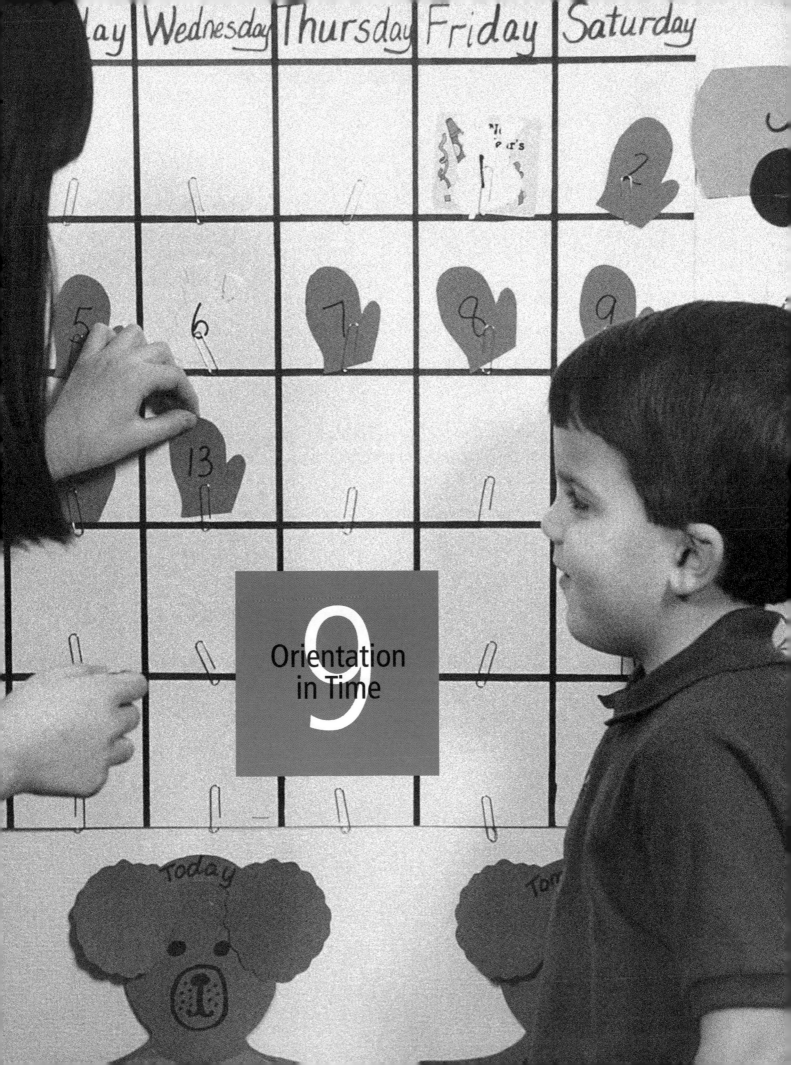

9

Orientation
in Time

Orientation in Time

OVERVIEW: The focus of this section is on the development of an inner sense of time; this orientation in time is essential not just as a reference point for future instruction in history, but also as another step towards personal autonomy, which requires that children be able to organize time, monitor behavior, and independently accomplish given activities throughout the day, week, and so on.

The child is asked first to organize and think about everyday experiences in regards to various indices of time: he or she is asked to classify experiences according to the time of day in which they occur, sequence events chronologically, and begin to use standard measures of time, such as daily schedules and calendars. The child is also asked to consider the passage of time on a larger scale, developing a sense of the relationship of past-present-future, by sequencing events in his or her own life, considering the relationships within his or her own family, as well as sequencing stages within the life cycle. He or she is also asked to assume an historical perspective outside of his or her immediate experiences by examining familiar contemporary objects with similar objects from the past. Finally, the child is asked to represent these experiences symbolically, both with words and schematically in timelines and drawings.

Goal: Understand and Use the Language of Time

LEVEL I	LEVEL II
• Understand and use the following vocabulary to describe day-to-day occurrences: (K) day-night; morning-afternoon-evening; today-tomorrow; before-after; first-last; now.	• Understand and use the following vocabulary to describe day-to-day occurrences: (K) yesterday-today-tomorrow; always-never-sometimes; immediately-in a little while-later; already; then; next; during; while; once upon a time; finally; soon.
	• Correctly use the present, past and future tense of verbs in describing day-to-day occurrences.

Goal: Establish Reference Points in Time

LEVEL I	LEVEL II
• Classify and describe images of everyday activities (waking up, eating breakfast, school, going to bed, etc.) according to the time of day with which they are associated: day-night; morning-afternoon-evening.	
• Sequence chronologically and describe 3 images of events or phases of a single event, occurring at temporally distinct times of the day that have been experienced.	
	• Sequence chronologically and describe 3-5 images of events or phases of a single event which have been experienced.

EXAMPLE: getting dressed, going to the park, eating dinner, etc.

EXAMPLE: steps in brushing teeth, making a cake, etc.

Goal: Establish Reference Points in Time, continued

LEVEL I	LEVEL II

LEVEL I

- Use the days of the week as a division of time: (K)

  - name the current day of the week.

- Identify the following by name: clock, daily schedule, calendar.

- Use a schedule of daily activities represented in images to describe the order of events for the day, i.e. which are the first and last activities.

- Use a weekly calendar to locate and name the current day of the week.

NOTE: The previous days of the month may be crossed out or marked in such a way as to aid the child in orienting himself to the calendar.

NOTE: Teacher provides correct monthly calendar in order for child to locate his or her date of birth.

LEVEL II

- Use the days of the week as a division of time: (K)

  - name the days of the week in sequence.

  - identify and distinguish the days of the week which make up the "weekend"

  - name the day that was "yesterday" and the day that will be "tomorrow."

- Use a year as a division of time:

  - name the current month.

  - name own date of birth (month and day).

- Use a schedule of daily activities represented in images to indicate which activity preceded and which will follow the current activity.

- Use a monthly calendar:

  - to locate and name the current day of the week (previous days marked or crossed out).

  - to name the current month.

  - to locate date of birth on a calendar of the appropriate month.

- Identify a horizontal series of 7 squares as representing one week on a monthly calendar.

- Name holidays and special events marked by symbols on a monthly calendar (name the event, describe whether it has already occurred or will occur later in the month).

Goal: Establish Reference Points in Time, continued

LEVEL I	LEVEL II
	• Use a time line:
	• to mark annual events: year long time line (seasons, holidays, family or classroom experiences, etc.)
	• to mark events across several lifetimes: century time line (birthdates of siblings, parents, grandparents, etc.)

Goal: Demonstrate an Awareness of the Passage of Time and of Periods of Time, as "The Past," "The Present," "The Future."

EXAMPLE: a class puppet show, construction of a building, etc.

NOTE: In all of the photo/drawing sequencing competencies, teacher may provide the photos and/or drawings; they need not be created by the child.

LEVEL I	LEVEL II
	• Sequence images depicting the evolution and completion of a project or undertaking, over an extended period of time – days, weeks, etc.
	• Sequence and describe photos and/or drawings that represent a timeline of one's own life and experiences.
	• Sequence photos and/or drawings of a baby, school-age child, young adult, elderly adult and describe in terms of:
	• the progression of the stages of development in the life of one person.
	• the generations within the context of a family (baby, child, parent, grandparent).
	• Arrange photos or drawings of members of his or her family on a genealogical tree or diagram to represent three generations:
	• self and siblings
	• parent(s)
	• grandparent(s)
	• Consider photos and/or drawings of activities associated with specific periods of life (infancy, childhood, young adulthood, old age) in reference to his or her present age/ stage of development (childhood), and indicate verbally whether these are activities that may be part of past, present or future experiences.

Goal: Demonstrate an Awareness of the Passage of Time and of Periods of Time, as "The Past," "The Present," "The Future," continued

LEVEL I	LEVEL II
	• Match images of contemporary objects with like objects from the past, indicating whether the objects belong to the "present" or "past" (clocks, telephones, cars, clothing, etc.)
	• Distinguish objects of the more "recent past" (occurring within the lifetime of the generations within his or her family) from objects of the "distant past" (long ago, a long time ago).

Language of Instruction

NOTE: For a full discussion, please see "Language of Instruction," in the Preschool Sequence Introduction and in the Implementation section.

TEACHER AND CHILDREN

REFERENCES IN TIME

after
afternoon
already
always
April
August
before
day
December
during
evening
February
finally
first
Friday
immediately
in a little while
January
July
June
last
later
long ao
March
May
Monday
month
morning
never
next
night

November
now
October
once upon a time
present
Saturday
September
sometimes
Sunday
then
Thursday
time
today
tomorrow
Tuesday
Wednesday
week
weekend
while
year

MEASURES OF TIME

calendar
clock
schedule
watch

PASSAGE OF TIME

a long time ago
change
long ago

TEACHER ONLY

REFERENCES IN TIME

century

MEASURES OF TIME

date
timeline

PASSAGE OF TIME

adult
age
baby
child
future
grow
old
past
the future
the past
the present
remember
young

EXAMPLE: Use vocabulary from the Orientation in Time section as follows:

CHILD: (showing photos brought from home) This is me when I was little.

ADULT: Let's look at them together. Can you tell me about each of these pictures that were taken when you were a *baby*?

CHILD: This is me in my crib. I'm drinking a bottle. This is me too.

ADULT: What were you doing in that picture?

CHILD: Don't know.

ADULT: It looks like you were crawling on the floor.

CHILD: Yeah – crawling. And this is me – outside.

ADULT: Ah, you were going for a ride in the stroller. Who is this *adult*? Who is pushing the stroller?

CHILD: Mommy.

ADULT: So when you were a *baby*, Mommy took you for a ride in the stroller? I'm glad you have these pictures of things that you did when you were a *baby*. They're things that already happened – they're things you did in the *past*. It's fun to remember things you did in the *past*. Can you *remember* any other things you did in the *past* when you were a *baby*?

CHILD: No.

ADULT: Here are some drawings of *babies* doing different things. Maybe, they'll help you remember something you did in the *past* when you were a *baby* (pointing). How about this?

CHILD: Diapers.

ADULT: When you were a *baby*, you wore diapers. That was something you did in the past. You don't wear diapers now!, etc.

10
Orientation in Space

Orientation in Space

OVERVIEW: The focus in this section is on the development of a sense of orientation in space, which enables the child to situate himself or herself in space in relation to his or her physical movements, as well as provides a context and vocabulary for later instruction in geometry and geography. The child is asked to situate first his or her own body, and then objects, in three dimensional space in relation to other objects, as well as to follow and give spatially referenced directions. He or she is asked to establish reference points in two dimensional space, copying various grid-like designs and completing mazes. The child is asked to demonstrate an understanding of several basic geographic features, such as ocean, mountain, island, and so on. Finally, he or she is asked to represent these experiences symbolically, both with words and schematically on maps and simple drawings.

Goal: Understand and Use the Language of Space

LEVEL I	LEVEL II
• Situate himself or herself in space or situate objects in relation to one another according to the following words: (K)	• Situate himself or herself in space or situate objects in relation to one another according to the following words: (K)
• there-here; near-far; next to-away from; in-on; in front of-behind; at the top-in the middle-at the bottom; to the side-in the middle; under; around; in a line/row; in a circle; up-down.	• in-on-outside; inside-outside; under-over; between; at the corner of; towards-against; before-after; above-below; high-low; left-right; face to face-back to back; front-back.

EXAMPLE: Go down the stairs. At the bottom of the stairs, turn down the hall that leads towards the playground. Go out the back door at the end of the hall to the playground.

• Follow or give oral, spatially referenced directions to move from one location to another, within a familiar environment.

NOTE: This competency represents a transition from actual experience and 3-D space to 2-D space which is represented on paper. Prior to tackling 2-D space as represented on paper, a child should have many experiences moving and orienting himself or herself in real space.

• Given oral, spatially referenced directions correlated to a picture in which different objects represent different "landmarks," trace the path described.

EXAMPLE: The old bear came out of his cave at the bottom of the mountain. He followed the path up the mountain between the pine trees. He crossed the river directly across from a small house and continued to the top of the mountain.

Goal: Establish Reference Points in Actual and Represented Space

NOTE This competency represents a transition from experience with manipulative objects and 3-D space to the representation of objects in 2-D space on paper. Prior to tackling 2-D space as represented on paper, a child should have many experiences using manipulative objects to copy designs, constructions, etc.

LEVEL I	LEVEL II
• Using parquetry blocks, pegboards and pegs or mosaic toys, reproduce a design/pattern by placing the pieces directly on top of the design/pattern card.	• Using parquetry blocks, pegboards and pegs or mosaic toys, reproduce a design/pattern represented on a separate design/pattern card.

• Using blocks of different shapes, colors and sizes, copy a tower or construction made by another person.

• Match halves of symmetrical objects to make a whole.

• Color squares on a blank grid to reproduce designs represented on other grids.

• Continue a linear frieze-like pattern of motifs/graphic symbols on a grid.

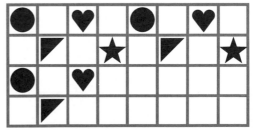

EXAMPLE: This is a game. There are three different columns, the heart, the star, the circle. Each has three different levels, red, yellow, blue. Use these clues to mark the right spot. Point to/ name the picture in the star column, on the red level (dog).

• Use simple coordinates to locate a point on a grid, in which points along the horizontal axis are designated by a motif and points along the vertical axis are designated by a color.

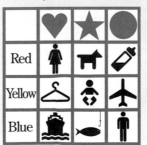

Goal: Establish Reference Points in Actual and Represented Space, continued

LEVEL I	LEVEL II
	• Use the shortest route to go from the exterior to the center of a simple maze.

Goal: Use Simple Maps of Familiar Environments (K)

LEVEL I	LEVEL II

• On a simple map of a single room showing furniture arrangements, etc., indicate his or her own position with an "x".	• On a simple map of a familiar space (home, school)
	
	  • mark the locations of specific objects, places, etc., as requested.
	
	  • mark with arrows or other symbols a path that has been taken from one place to another.

Goal: Demonstrate an Understanding of Basic Geographic Concepts

LEVEL I	LEVEL II
• Identify the following geographic features and environments by name in "real life," photos or drawings: land, water, river, lake, ocean, farm, countryside.	• Identify the following geographic features and environments by name in "real life," photos or drawings: mountain, island, forest (woods), jungle, city.
	• Name the city, state and country in which he or she lives. (K)

	• Identify a map of the United States, indicating: (K)
	
	  • the location of his or her state.
	
	  • land and ocean areas.

	• Identify a globe by name, indicating land and ocean areas. (K)

Language of Instruction

REFERENCE POINTS IN SPACE		REFERENCE POINTS IN SPACE

NOTE: For a full discussion, please see "Language of Instruction," in the Preschool Sequence Introduction and in the Implementation section.

REFERENCE POINTS IN SPACE (Teacher and Children)

above	outside	design
after	over	directions
against	right	graph paper
around	there	grid
at the bottom	to the side	half
at the corner	towards	maze
at the top	under	path
away from		pattern
back	**MAPS**	place
back-to-back	country	route
before	globe	space
behind	land	whole
below	map	
between	ocean	
face-to-face	state	
far	United States	
front		
here		
high	**GEOGRAPHIC CONCEPTS**	
in	city	
in a line/row	countryside	
in a circle	farm	
in front of	forest	
in the middle	island	
inside	jungle	
left	lake	
low	ocean	
near	river	
next to	woods	
on		

EXAMPLE: Use vocabulary from the Orientation in Space section as follows:

CHILD: Look what I made.

ADULT: What did you make?

CHILD: I colored.

ADULT: Yes, you made a very pretty *design* on the *graph paper*. In your *design*, did you use the same color or a different color for each little box?

CHILD: Different colors.

ADULT: Your design is very colorful because you used a lot of different colors – each box is different. Danny made a design on *graph paper* today, too. Maybe tomorrow you can exchange *designs* – you can see if you can copy Danny's *design* and he can try to copy your *design*.

11
Scientific Reasoning and the Physical World

Scientific Reasoning and the Physical World

OVERVIEW: This section introduces children to a systematic way of looking at, describing, and explaining the world around them. Children should be given many opportunities for systematic observation and hands-on investigation of both the living and material world. Building on these experiences, children can progress from describing and explaining what is observed to making predictions based on these observations.

This systematic approach may be summarized as: (1) observe, (2) gather background information (using nonfiction books, films/videos, photos, etc., as sources), (3) predict, (4) observe again, and (5) represent findings (words, drawings, displays, photos, etc.).

It is worth emphasizing that the final step, documenting and representing observations and findings, is an especially important part of this process. In so doing, children may be guided in making the important transition and connection between "hands-on" investigation to symbolic representation. At the preschool level, keep in mind that a "picture is worth a thousand words": reporting of observations may often be more readily accomplished through drawings completed by the children, selection and display of objects or photographs, in addition to verbal explanations. This representational step will also enhance young children's appreciation of science as "telling the story about how nature works."

The goals here ask children to describe key physical characteristics, needs, and the basic life cycle of plants and animals, including man, as well as identify basic properties of water, air, and light. They are also asked to demonstrate how to use a variety of everyday tools.

Goal: Demonstrate an Initial Understanding of the Living World

LEVEL I	LEVEL II
• Identify and describe key physical and sensory characteristics of humans, as well as human needs, stages of development, and life cycle.	• Identify and describe key physical and sensory characteristics of humans, as well as human needs, stages of development, and life cycle.
• Identify and describe objects on the basis of specific properties discerned through the five senses:	
• sight: see Mathematical Reasoning and Number Sense.	
• taste: sweet, sour, salty, identification of specific flavors.	
• hearing: see Music.	
• touch: hard-soft, rough-smooth, wet-dry, flexible-stiff.	
• smell: identification of environmental scents.	

EXAMPLE: identification of environmental scents, flower, smoke, baking bread, etc.

84

Goal: Demonstrate an Initial Understanding of the Living World, continued

LEVEL I

- Identify basic body parts: see Autonomy.

EXAMPLE: recognizing a song – ear/hear; feeling a mosquito bite – skin/touch; recognizing a mother's perfume – nose/smell (K)

EXAMPLE: identify healthy foods.

EXAMPLE: associate appropriate clothing with different weather conditions.

EXAMPLE: children's drawings, photo displays, and oral descriptions of: **the animal's physical appearance, growth/ development**, including any changes over time, **sensory perceptions and organs**: comparison to human senses, ie. does the animal see, smell, hear, etc. and how?, **food and drink:** how the animal eats, **habitat:** specific conditions necessary for **growth and survival**, **natural protection:** how the animal defends itself; sequential arrangements of photos or drawings to depict the **life cycle**.

LEVEL II

- Identify basic organs, their location and function:
  - heart – beats to make blood flow/circulate.
  - lungs – air taken in through nose fills lungs to breathe.

- Identify the sense and body part associated with the awareness/experience of certain sensations.

- Identify and describe basic needs:
  - food and drink.
  - shelter and protection from temperature and weather.

- Sequence photos and/or drawings of a baby, school-age child, young adult, elderly adult to represent the life cycle, describing stages of development, changes in physical appearance (height, weight, hair, teeth, etc.).

- Care for, observe, and record observations of an animal, noting key physical characteristics, development, needs, and life cycle. (K)

Goal: Demonstrate an Initial Understanding of the Living World, continued

LEVEL I	LEVEL II
	• Classify images of animals according to the habitat or environment in which they generally live: lake/river, ocean, farm, forest (woods), jungle.
EXAMPLE: use children's drawings, photo displays, and oral descriptions of **parts of the plant**: seed, roots, stem, leaves, flower, fruit; **conditions needed for growth**: light, water, heat, soil; **growth and development**: initial sprouting, development of roots and shoots, increase in size.; sequential arrangements of photos or drawings to depict the **life cycle**.	• Plant, care for, observe, and record observations of a plant, noting the parts of the plant, needs, development and its life cycle (K).

Goal: Demonstrate an Initial Understanding of Elements of the Material World

LEVEL I	LEVEL II
EXAMPLE: observe the effects of **temperature** on the states of water: solid, liquid, gas.; identify examples of the different **states of water within the natural world**; observe the principles of **flotation** and **dissolution** of various substances that are placed in water.	• Observe, describe, and record some basic properties of water, its presence and effects in the physical world.
EXAMPLE: experience and describe the ways one can identify, observe and feel the **presence of air (wind)** in the natural world; identify and classify **objects that use air/wind** (sailboat, pinwheel, windmill, kite, etc.) and **objects that produce air/wind** (fans, hair dryer, bellows, etc.)	• Observe, describe, and record some basic properties of air, its presence and effects in the physical world.
EXAMPLE: identify the **sun** as a source of natural light in the physical world; use natural and artificial light sources to produce **shadows** and examine different effects.	• Observe, describe, and record some basic properties of light, its presence and effects in the physical world.

Goal: Use Tools and Objects to Construct and Create

LEVEL I	LEVEL II
	• Select and use the appropriate cooking utensil for a particular task, in carrying out a simple recipe.

EXAMPLE: **mix:** spoon, spatula, electric beater, blender; **cut, chop:** knife, blender; **flatten, roll:** rolling pin; **drain:** colander.

LEVEL I	LEVEL II
• Select and use the appropriate tool to complete a particular task as part of a project or activity:	• Select and use the appropriate tool to complete a particular task as part of a project or activity:
• cut: scissors (straight lines).	• cut: scissors (curved lines).
	• join paper: stapler.
	• join fabric: needle and thread.
	• join wood: nail, hammer.
	• dig a hole: trowel, shovel.
	• water a plant: watering can, hose.
	• Create or construct an object.

NOTE: Large, blunt needles, such as those used in darning, may be used with a loose woven fabric, such as burlap.

EXAMPLE: build a balanced tower of blocks; make a vehicle which rolls, using interlocking blocks; using scrap materials, make a boat that floats; make a pinwheel.

Language of Instruction

NOTE: For a full discussion, please see "Language of Instruction," in the Preschool Sequence Introduction and in the Implementation section.

TEACHER AND CHILDREN		TEACHER ONLY	
ANIMALS	**PLANTS**	**ANIMALS**	**MATERIAL WORLD**
air	air	birth	ice
alive	alive	development	light source
animal	bulb	flow	liquid
blood	flower	growth	shadow
breathe	fruit	life cycle	solid
farm	grow	sense	state
forest	leaf	temperature	steam
grow	light	weather	
hearing	living		**GENERAL**
heart	plant	**PLANTS**	describe
jungle	roots	development	explain
lake	seed	growth	observation
living	stem	life cycle	observe
lungs	water	shoot	record
move		soil	report
ocean	**MATERIAL WORLD**	sprout	predict
river	air	temperature	science
salty	alive	weather	
smell	light		**TOOLS/CONSTRUCT**
sour	living	**MATERIAL WORLD**	build
sweet	not living	boil	construct
taste	sun	dissolve	create
touch	water	float	tool
water	wind	freeze	utensil
		gas	
		heat	

EXAMPLE: Use vocabulary from the Scientific Reasoning and the Physical World section as follows:

CHILD: Oh, look – there are green things coming out of the dirt!

ADULT: Ah, you're right! I see a little green *stem*. Look carefully – what do these two little things on the top of the *stem* look like?

CHILD: Other parts.

ADULT: Yes, each one is a little *leaf*. Can you gently point to the *leaf* on each side of the *stem*?

CHILD: Here and here?

ADULT: That's right, those are the *leaves*. Now, where do you suppose the *stem* came from? How did it get here in the *soil*?

CHILD: (silence)

ADULT: Do you remember what you *planted* in the *soil* a couple of days ago?

CHILD: A *seed*.

ADULT: That's right. Look at the drawings you've made so far to *record* your *observations*. See, in the first picture, you drew a picture of the *seed* in the *soil*. Tell me about this next picture. What did you draw?

CHILD: It's the *seed* in the dirt. I'm giving it some *water*.

ADULT: (pointing) What else is the *seed* getting in your picture?

CHILD: The *sun*.

ADULT: Right. The *sun* and *water* made this green *stem grow* from the *seed*. Do you think it would be a good idea to draw another picture of your *observations* today?

12

Music

Music

OVERVIEW: This section includes goals that focus both on listening to, enjoying, and appreciating music in all its various forms, as well as producing music. Experiences in listening to and singing songs and fingerplays also provide opportunities to practice oral language skills. Music affords the opportunity to expand and clarify various concepts, such as "loud, soft," "fast, slow," etc. In addition, efforts that focus attention on discriminating differences in discrete environmental or musical sounds facilitate subsequent attention to phonemic awareness, awareness of the discrete sounds of language. Group musical experiences, performing or singing together, also offer the opportunity to practice social skills.

The basic goals of this section ask the child to listen to and identify sounds, indicate whether certain sound pairs are the same or different, imitate sounds and rhythm sequences, sing songs individually and with others, and move interpretatively to music.

Goal: Listen to and Discriminate Differences in Sound

LEVEL I	LEVEL II
• Identify the direction from which a sound originates.	
• Listen to environmental sounds and identify the sound.	
• Listen to pairs of sounds that are either identical or grossly different and indicate whether they are the "same" or "different". Sound pairs that are "different" should be created by different objects/ instruments.	
	• Listen to pairs of sounds that are either identical or different (but similar) and indicate whether they are the "same" or "different." Sound pairs that are different may be created by different but similar sounding objects/instruments or by the same object/instrument, but vary in intensity (loud,soft), pitch (high,low), or duration (long,short).
• Indicate the number of sounds heard (environmental sounds, rhythm band instruments, claps, etc.), up to 4 sounds.	
	• Identify family members or friends by their voice alone.
	• Listen to environmental sounds presented sequentially as a "sound story" and describe the events and context in which they are occurring.

EXAMPLE: a bird singing, a car motor, water running, etc.

EXAMPLE: sounds that are different: bell-whistle, drawer closing- water running, drum-triangle.

EXAMPLE: similar sounding objects/instruments: maracas-sand-paper blocks, bell-triangle, two notes on the ends of the scale on a xylophone, etc

EXAMPLE: someone getting up in the morning (yawning, washing face, brushing teeth, getting dressed, etc.).

Goal: Listen to and Discriminate Differences in Sound, continued

LEVEL I	LEVEL II
	• Identify and associate sounds with the instruments and objects which produce them (when the instruments and objects are heard, but hidden from sight), such as:
EXAMPLE: whistle, bell, horn.	◦ objects.
EXAMPLE: triangle, tambourine, maracas, rhythm sticks, drum.	◦ rhythm band instruments.
	◦ piano, violin. (K)
	• Identify a selection of music as either vocal or instrumental.

Goal: Imitate and Produce Sounds

LEVEL I	LEVEL II
• Vocally or with musical instruments, produce sounds that are loud or soft, long or short, according to verbal direction.	
• Vocally imitate isolated sounds produced by others, approximating intensity, duration, and pitch.	
• Imitate clapping pattern sequences of no more than 3 claps/pattern.	• Imitate clapping pattern sequences of at least 4 claps/pattern, which are more complex in varying tempo, the number and length of pauses between claps, etc.
• Use musical instruments or other objects to imitate a sequence of no more than 3 sounds/musical motifs, made by one instrument/object.	• Use musical instruments or other objects to imitate a sequence of 3 or more sounds made by more than one instrument.
• Accompany a story or musical piece by introducing sound effects (environmental or animal sounds, a musical instrument, etc.) at the appropriate moment, using sound effects that have been previously introduced by an adult.	• Accompany a story or musical piece by introducing sound effects (environmental or animal sounds, a musical instrument, etc.) at the appropriate moment, inventing one's own sound effects, after having listened to the story.
	• Accompany an adult by either clapping or using rhythm instruments to maintain the beat in a chant, song, or other musical piece. (K)

Goal: Listen to and Sing Songs

LEVEL I	LEVEL II
• Listen to, sing, and perform children's songs and fingerplays with others.	• Listen to, sing, and perform children's songs and fingerplays individually or with others.

EXAMPLE: Did You Ever See a Lassie, Lazy Mary, Oh, Do You Know the Muffin Man?

• Sing a musical dialogue in which two or more groups answer one another.

EXAMPLE: Row, Row, Row Your Boat, Are You Sleeping?

• Sing a round for two groups.

NOTE: For musical dialogues and rounds, the emphasis for preschoolers is on having fun with language and music, not on a flawless rendition of the song.

Fingerplays and Songs:

The following titles represent a core of traditional songs and fingerplays for young children. They will enjoy listening to and singing these selections. Teachers and parents are encouraged to supplement these recommendations with additional selections from popular, contemporary children's music.

A Tisket, A Tasket
Are You Sleeping?
Bingo (K)
Blue-Tail Fly (Jimmie Crack Corn)
Do Your Ears Hang Low?
Did You Ever See a Lassie?
Eensy, Weensy Spider
Five Little Ducks That I Once Knew
Five Little Monkeys Jumping On the Bed
Happy Birthday to You
Head and Shoulders, Knees and Toes
Here is the Beehive
Hush Little Baby (K)
I Know an Old Lady
If You're Happy and You Know It (K)
I'm a Little Teapot
John Jacob Jingleheimer Schmidt (K)
Kookaburra
Lazy Mary
Looby Loo
Oats, Peas, Beans and Barley Grow
Oh, Dear What Can the Matter Be? (1)
Oh, Do You Know the Muffin Man?
Oh Where, Oh Where, Has My Little Dog Gone?
Old MacDonald (K)
One Potato, Two Potato
Open, Shut Them
Pop Goes the Weasel

Fingerplays and Songs, continued:
 Row, Row, Row Your Boat (1)
 Teddy Bear, Teddy Bear, Turn Around
 Teddy Bears' Picnic
 The Wheels on the Bus (K)
 Twinkle, Twinkle, Little Star (K)
 Where is Thumbkin?
 Who Stole the Cookie from the Cookie Jar?
 Yankee Doodle (1)
 You Are My Sunshine.

Goal: Listen to and Move to Music of Different Styles and Periods

LEVEL I	LEVEL II
• Move to music:	• Move to music:
• individually, interpreting and modifying one's movements according to the tempo (slow-fast), intensity (loud-soft), and rhythm of the music.	• individually, interpreting and modifying one's movements according to the tempo (slow-fast), intensity (loud-soft), and rhythm of the music.
• performing very simple movements, with a partner or group, in accompaniment to the music.	
	• carrying out a sequence of choreographed steps or movements to music.

EXAMPLE: perform simple movements: partners clap hands together during refrain, and during remainder of music, hold hands and turn in a circle.

EXAMPLE: carry out choreographed steps: Children's Polka, Danish Dance of Greeting.

Suggested Instrumental Works:

In addition to the recommended songs and fingerplays, popular children's and instrumental music and music from other cultures, the following works, all with strong melody and rhythm, are recommended for listening and creative movement. While teachers and parents are encouraged to refer to the works by title and/or composer, preschool children are not expected to identify works or composers by name.

 Georges Bizet, Overture to *Carmen*
 Johannes Brahms, "Cradle Song" ("Brahms' Lullaby")
 Claude Debussy, "Cakewalk" from *Children's Corner Suite*
 Victor Herbert, "March of the Toys" from *Babes in Toyland*
 Aram Khachaturian, "Sabre Dance" from *Gayane*
 Wolfgang Amadeus Mozart, Variations on "Ah, vous dirai-je maman!"
 Jacques Offenbach, "Can-can" from *Gaite parisienne*
 Amilcare Ponchielli, "Dance of the Hours"
 Robert Schumann, "Dreams" from *Scenes from Childhood*
 Johann Strauss, Jr., "Donner und Blitz" ("Thunder and Lightning") waltz
 Peter Ilich Tchaikovsky, from *The Nutcracker*, "March," "Dance of the Flutes," and "Dance of the Sugar Plum Fairies" (1)
 Heitor Villa-Lobos, "The Little Train of Caipira"

Language of Instruction

NOTE: For a full discussion, please see "Language of Instruction," in the Preschool Sequence Introduction and in the Implementation section.

TEACHER AND CHILDREN	TEACHER ONLY	
different	beat	rhythm band
fast	clap	instruments
high	clapping pattern	rhythm sticks
listen	composer	round
long	copy	sing
loud	drum	solo
low	fingerplay	sound
music	imitate	sound effects
piano	instrument	tambourine
same	instrumental	triangle
short	maracas	verse
sing	melody	vocal music
slow	musician	voice
soft	orchestra	
song	refrain	
violin	repeat	
	rhythm	

EXAMPLE: Use vocabulary from the Music section as follows:

ADULT: *Listen* – I'm going to *clap* my hands – I'm going to make a *clapping pattern*. *Listen* carefully. When I finish, I'm going to ask you to try to *copy* it. (clap pattern)

ADULT: Okay, I'm going to *repeat* the *clapping pattern*, but this time, you try to do it with me. (adult and child clap together)

ADULT: Now I'm going to make a new *clapping pattern*. *Listen* carefully. When I finish, I will ask you to *repeat* it by yourself.

13

Visual Arts

Visual Arts

OVERVIEW: This section focuses not only on producing art, but also on examining and appreciating examples of various art forms. The use of various media and techniques provides rich opportunities for sensory exploration and manipulation, as well as the development of fine motor skills. In addition, through painting and drawing, children make their first attempts at graphic representation, a precursor to writing. The guided examination of works of art provides practice in focusing attention on visual detail, important for developing skill in discriminating visual differences in objects, images, print, and letters, as well as appreciating basic elements of art. The further examination and discussion of works of art also afford rich opportunities for language development.

The basic goals of this section ask children to attend to visual details, identify images that are the same or different, create both representational and nonrepresentational art using various media and techniques, create art in the style of a known artist, and examine and talk about selected works of art, including their own creations.

Goal: Attend to Visual Detail of Objects and Images

	LEVEL I	LEVEL II
EXAMPLE: See Mathematical Reasoning and Number Sense .	• Identify pairs of objects or images as the "same" or "different."	
	• Play games requiring matching of like images, such as lotto games.	• Play games requiring matching of like images, such as domino games.
EXAMPLE: sky-blue, grass-green, cloud-white, leaf-green (or red, yellow, orange, brown).	• Identify the following colors: red, yellow, green, blue, orange, purple, brown, black, white.	• Identify from memory the color of objects from nature, when not in view.
	• Demonstrate memory of visual details by identifying what is different after a collection of objects is examined, removed from sight, altered, and then reintroduced.	• Demonstrate memory of visual details by playing "Concentration" memory games or describing a picture that has been removed from view.

Goal: Explore and Create, Using Various Art Forms, Media, and Techniques.

	LEVEL I	LEVEL II
NOTE: Large blunt needles, such as those used in darning, may be used with a loose woven fabric, such as burlap.	• Use various tools and techniques in completing art projects: tear, fold, paste, tape, use stickers, cut straight lines with scissors.	• Use various tools and techniques in completing art projects: staple, cut straight or curved lines or corners with scissors, sew using basting or overcast stitch.

Goal: Explore and Create, Using Various Art Forms, Media, and Techniques, continued

LEVEL I	LEVEL II

EXAMPLE: Children may use various media, including: **Printing:** paint, ink – sponges, objects, stamps; **Painting:** fingerpaints, tempera, watercolor – fingers, brush, assorted objects, such as, a feather, comb, string, straw, etc.; **Drawing:** pencil, crayon, marker, chalk; **Collage:** torn paper (tissue paper, construction paper, magazine photos...), objects (buttons, seeds...); **Sculpture:** clay, wood scraps.

LEVEL I

- Create nonrepresentational and representational works, such as printing, painting, drawing, collage, and sculpture.

LEVEL II

- Create nonrepresentational and representational works, such as printing, painting, drawing, collage, and sculpture.

- Examine a work of art by a known artist and create a work "in the style of" the work examined. (K)

Recommended Works:
Sonia Delaunay, *Rhythm*
Egyptian Dynasty, *Blue Hippo* (faience sculpture)
Paul Klee, *Head of a Man (Senecio)* (7)
Henri Matisse, *Red Interior, Blue Table*
Henri Matisse, *The Snail* (collage) (2)
Joan Miro, *People and Dog in Sun*
Piet Mondrian, *Broadway Boogie-Woogie* (7)

- Work with other children to create a collective work of art, such as a large group mural, collage, sculpture, etc.

Goal: Develop an Appreciation for Art

LEVEL I	LEVEL II
	• Look at and talk about works of art, describing the details and "story" depicted, such as, objects, people, activities, setting, time of day/year, long ago-contemporary, etc., as well as the mood/feeling that certain pieces of art elicit.

Recommended Works:
Romare Bearden, *Summertime*
Edgar Degas, *Little Fourteen Year Old Dancer* (1) (bronze sculpture)
Edward Hicks, *Noah's Ark*
Jonathan Eastman Johnson, *The Old Stagecoach*
Munier, *Special Moment*
Horace Pippin, *Domino Players*
Henri Rousseau, *The Sleeping Gypsy*

	• Describe his or her own art work, explaining the materials and technique(s) used.

Language of Instruction

NOTE: For a full discussion, please see "Language of Instruction," in the Preschool Sequence Introduction and in the Implementation section.

TEACHER AND CHILDREN		TEACHER ONLY	
art	scissors	artist	mural
black	tape	brush	museum
blue	triangle	chalk	original
brown	white	collage	painter
circle	yellow	compare	painting
color		copy	print
cut		create	real
different		creativity	remember
draw		curved line	sculptor
glue		detail	sculpture
green		easel	shape
orange		feelings	staple
paint		fold	straight line
paste		imaginary	tear
purple		imagination	technique
rectangle		line	title
red		materials	tool
same		mood	

EXAMPLE: Use vocabulary from the Visual Arts section as follows:

ADULT: This is a picture of a *sculpture* that was *created* by the *artist* Edgar Degas. Can you tell me about this *sculpture*? What do you see?

CHILD: It's a person.

ADULT: Uh-huh, it's a *sculpture* of a person. What kind of person? Is it a man or woman? Or a girl or boy?

CHILD: It looks like a girl 'cause she has a pony tail.

ADULT: So it's a sculpture of a girl. How is she dressed? Is she wearing regular clothes?

CHILD: No – she looks like she's wearing a funny short skirt.

ADULT: Yes, she is. She's wearing a special costume that's used for dancing, etc.

implementation

Long-Term Planning: The Preschool Sequence Month-by-Month

Organizing and Integrating: The Preschool Sequence and the Daily Schedule

Scaffolding Learning: Guiding Young Children to Increasing Competency

Language of Instruction: How to Incorporate into Daily Lessons

Sample Lessons: Math Exploration in a Pre-Kindergarten Classroom

Resources and Materials: Tools for Implementing the Preschool Sequence

Long Term
Planning:
The Preschool
Sequence
Month-
by-Month

Long Term Planning: The Preschool Sequence Month-by-Month

Once you decide that you would like to incorporate the Core Knowledge Preschool Sequence into your class or preschool program, it will be helpful to set aside time for some in-depth planning. Ideally, if more than one teacher/class will use the Preschool Sequence in your setting, this planning should be a cooperative effort involving all teachers.

One of the principal goals of this planning should be to "take apart" the Preschool Sequence and develop a month-by-month planning guide. If your setting offers only one year of preschool for four-five year-olds, you should develop a one year, month-by- month plan. If your setting also offers preschool for three year-olds, you should develop a two year, month-by-month plan, one for three-four year-olds and one for four-five year-olds.

Some schools choose to begin by representing the various components associated with pre-existing district/state guidelines or local programs, month-by-month. The Preschool Sequence can then be integrated into this outline, month-by-month.

Other schools choose to begin the planning process using the Preschool Sequence as the initial foundation for the month-by-month plan, adding local or state guidelines later. If your local or state guidelines are vague or ambiguous, it may be easier to begin the planning process in this way.

Month-by-month planning guides will vary considerably between preschool settings; there is no one single way to organize and present the Preschool Sequence month-by-month. As you and your colleagues discuss and decide when to present and teach particular parts of the Preschool Sequence, you should keep the following in mind:

From easy to complex

The competencies and skills listed within each subject area and/or subtopic of an area in the Preschool Sequence, such as mathematical reasoning, are generally listed sequentially, from easy to more complex. The order in which these skills are presented, combined with your prior knowledge and experience in working with preschool children, should assist you in deciding "what to teach when." For example, as suggested by the order of the competencies in the Preschool Sequence, you would want to plan experiences with patterning using concrete objects prior to planning experiences in which children create patterns on paper.

Mastery takes persistence

As you begin to note skills and competencies on your month-by-month guide, you will realize that some skills will involve ongoing experiences that will need to be practiced over several months before the skills are mastered. It is recommended that you note such skills in the given month that they will first be presented, recognizing that skills will not necessarily be mastered in the same month that they are first presented. Indeed, it is expected that, as in any effective teaching setting, the teacher will monitor student performance and extend opportunities for practice in subsequent months.

It is particularly noteworthy that the nature of some skills and competencies, especially those in the areas of Autonomy/Social Skills and Oral Language, are such that practice and experiences will need to be ongoing throughout the entire year, each month. It may be helpful to indicate "all year" in association with each of these skills on the monthly guide (see sample guides that follow) to serve as a reminder of the ongoing nature of these skills, even though they will only be noted during the first month in which they are presented.

Timing

Decisions about when to present certain content, such as particular nursery rhymes, stories, songs, etc., can be made with great flexibility, keeping in mind only that some rhymes and stories are shorter and less complex than others, for example, and perhaps put to better use in the earlier months of the year. As you select rhymes, stories, songs, science topics, music and artwork from the Preschool Sequence for certain months, you might want to consider holidays and traditions that are generally associated with particular months, as well as other themes that you may typically incorporate at certain times of the year.

Within preschool settings with two year programs, it will be helpful for the preschool teachers to come to a consensus, in keeping with their own program needs, about which particular rhymes, stories, songs, etc., from the Preschool Sequence will be presented at Level I and which at Level II.

Incorporating it into your program

Do keep in mind that if your setting offers only one year of preschool for four- to five-year-old children, as noted in the introductory questions and answers section, you will use the Level II material from the Preschool Sequence as you plan your month-by-month guide. However, you will also need to be very familiar with the Level I material, recognizing when it is important to incorporate some prerequisite Level I skills and competencies prior to introducing certain Level II material.

Another consideration in a one year program will be the need to incorporate all the content, that is, nursery rhymes, stories, songs, etc., from the Preschool Sequence in one year, instead of interspersing it over a two year period.

Once the year-long month-by-month guide is completed, it is anticipated that each teacher will focus on one month at a time, starting with September, to guide the more detailed planning of centers and specific activities for that month. You will undoubtedly add other experiences, activities, rhymes, stories, songs, and so on, each month, based upon your children's and your own interests and preferences. However, it is important to think of your month-by-month guide as the basic foundation of your program.

The following pages present sample month-by-month guides for both Level I and Level II of the Preschool Sequence. Don't forget that these represent just one of many, many possible ways to organize the material included in the Preschool Sequence. Different teachers and preschools will come up with a variety of effective ways to incorporate the Preschool Sequence in their setting.

NOTE: In the sample month-by-month guides that follow, the Level II guide has been developed on the assumption that it is part of a two-year program. That is, the sample Level II guide assumes that children have been exposed to certain rhymes, stories and music from the Preschool Sequence as specified in the Level I programming.

NOTE: Some preschool teachers may find this notion of planning to be a very new concept. For many, many years, accepted early childhood theory and practice stipulated that children constructed their knowledge of the world individually, without influence from others. Planning was deemed inappropriate, if not impossible, in that learning was to be only child-initiated. Given current research (see Appendix B, "Developmentally Appropriate Practice: What Have We Learned?," for a more thorough discussion), we now know that a more balanced approach is necessary—teachers can be sensitive to children's spontaneous interests and provide time to explore those interests, while still planning other experiences and activities that are deemed essential to the development of all children.

For a very practical example of how to incorporate children's interests and still use the month-by-month plan to guide your instruction, perhaps, as in the sample plan that follows, you have decided that in the area of Scientific Reasoning, you will focus on the human body during the month of September. However, when school starts, you have a child who is "wildly enthusiastic, can't stop talking" about his new pet kitten. To capitalize upon all the children's evident interest, you decide to postpone the human body activities that you had planned and instead introduce activities on observing and caring for animals, originally slated to be introduced in October. This is fine! What is important is to be certain to reinsert the body activities, actually noting it as part of the plan in another month, as soon as you decide to make a change. That way, you won't inadvertently forget about it.

Ultimately, the point of the month-by-month plan is not to unflinchingly adhere to what you originally set out in writing. As the year progresses, you may find any number of very good reasons to modify the original plan and shift some things from one month to another. The purpose of the plan is to make sure that this is done in a conscious and deliberate way that ensures that the essential experiences of the Preschool Sequence will not be omitted.

Level One: **Month-by-Month Guide**

SEPTEMBER

Movement
attention: stop-start with signal

Autonomy/Social Skills
name recognition: oral and written
body parts: face
teacher and classmates by name
sit among others; stay in own space
(all year)
carry out chores and responsibili-
ties (all year)

Oral Language
adapt volume of voice
object/person/picture match with
description

**Nursery Rhymes, Poems,
Fingerplays, Songs**
memorize and recite nursery
rhymes (all year)
perform hand and body gestures
with rhymes (all year)
Rhymes: Pat-A-Cake
This Little Piggy Went to Market
Happy Birthday
Rain, Rain Go Away

**Storybook Reading and
Storytelling**
listen to picture books read aloud
(all year)
find the object/illustration being
described
Story: Three Little Pigs

**Emerging Literacy Skills in
Reading and Writing**
recognize written first name
(all year)
small muscle control activities
(all year)
tear, fold and paste

Mathematical Reasoning
pairs of objects/pictures as same
or different

Orientation in Time and Space
space: in a line/row

Scientific Reasoning
identify body parts: face

Music
sound localization

Visual Arts
collage (all year)
tear, paste
Colors: red, blue

OCTOBER

Movement
up/down steps
balance: change body position,
same space

Autonomy/Social Skills
body parts: body
good hygiene (all year)
acknowledge and return greetings,
farewells (all year)
wait turn to speak (all year)
stop when told; change activities
(all year)

Work Habits
put away toys and materials
(all year)

Oral Language
describe attributes of object/
person/picture
express personal needs, desires
(all year)

**Nursery Rhymes, Poems,
Fingerplays, Songs**
Rhymes: Head and Shoulders,
Knees and Toes
Jack-O-Lantern
Where is Thumbkin?
Open, Shut Them
Rock-A-Bye Baby

**Storybook Reading and
Storytelling**
hold book correctly, turn pages
describe an illustration

Story: Goldilocks & the Three
Bears

**Emerging Literacy Skills in
Reading and Writing**
produce written marks (lines,
scribbles) on horizontal, vertical
surfaces

Mathematical Reasoning
sort by color

Orientation in Time and Space
time: day-night; morning-afternoon-
evening
time: classify, describe activities
according to the time of day

Scientific Reasoning
identify body parts: body

Music
pairs of sounds as same
or different
Instrumental Works: Brahms,
Cradle Song

Visual Arts
painting (all year)
Colors: yellow, green

NOVEMBER

Movement
balance: walk forward on beam
throw/kick object
Game: Ring Around the Rosie

Autonomy/Social Skills
draw stick figure (all year)
attend and listen while others
speak (all year)
table manners (all year)
greet adults: Mr., Mrs., Ms.
(all year)

Oral Language
describe event or task as it is
taking place

**Nursery Rhymes, Poems,
Fingerplays, Songs**
Rhymes: Ring Around the Rosie

CONTINUED NEXT PAGE

Diddle, Diddle Dumpling,
My Son John
Teddy Bear, Teddy Bear
Two Little Blackbirds

**Storybook Reading and
Storytelling**
Stories: The Lion & Mouse
Thanksgiving Day celebration

**Emerging Literacy Skills in
Reading and Writing**
paste stickers on horizontal,
vertical lines, spiral

Mathematical Reasoning
match shapes to outlines
sort by shape
identify circles by name

Orientation in Time and Space
time: name the current day of the
week (all year)
time: use a schedule of daily
activities to describe order of
events
space: in a circle

Scientific Reasoning
describe objects using the senses:
vision

Music
identify environmental sounds

Visual Arts
use stickers (all year)
Colors: orange, brown

DECEMBER
Movement
situate self within space of defined
boundaries
move through space in different
ways; no obstacles
throw/kick object (all year)
Game: London Bridge

Autonomy/Social Skills
put on clothing
make/acknowledge requests
politely (all year)

Oral Language
carry on a conversation with adult
(all year)

describe an event in the immediate
past
use present and past verb tense
(all year)
understand and use increasingly
elaborate declarative sentences
(all year)

**Nursery Rhymes, Poems,
Fingerplays, Songs**
Rhymes: Lucy Locket
Pease Porridge Hot
Polly Put the Kettle On
Old MacDonald

**Storybook Reading and
Storytelling**
repeat/provide refrain (all year)
Stories: Gingerbread Boy
Brown Bear, Brown Bear

**Emerging Literacy Skills in
Reading and Writing**
identify examples of print (all year)
collect objects using illustrated list

Mathematical Reasoning
member/group - does an object
belong to a group?
copy a pattern of 6-10 objects,
alternate one property
match objects to pattern cards
recite the number sequence, 1-4
(all year)

Orientation in Time and Space
time: before-after
space: there-here, near-far, in-on
space: land-water

Scientific Reasoning
describe objects using senses: taste

Music
sing a musical dialogue in which
two or more groups answer
one another
move to music individually,
interpreting and modifying
movements according to tempo,
intensity and rhythm (all year)
Instrumental Works: Tchaikovsky,
The Nutcracker

Visual Arts
play matching lotto games

sculpture: clay or play doh
(all year)
Color: purple

JANUARY
Movement
move through obstacle courses
(all year)
play catch with bean bag (all year)
imitate position/single action
of another
Game: Follow the Leader

Work Habits
choose and use toy/activity
independently (all year)

Oral Language
answer telephone
sequence and describe 3 images
of events that have been
experienced at temporally
distinct times of the day
ask or answer questions beginning
with who, what, where, when,
why (all year)

**Nursery Rhymes, Poems,
Fingerplays, Songs**
clap/tap the beat of a nursery
rhyme (all year)
Rhymes: One For The Money
Higglety, Pigglety, Pop!
Here is the Beehive
Lazy Mary

**Storybook Reading and
Storytelling**
answer questions about the
characters, setting, plot and
events of a story (all year)
Stories: Curious George
Make Way for Ducklings
The Snowy Day

**Emerging Literacy Skills in
Reading and Writing**
color a simple drawing (all year)
writing strokes: horizontal,
vertical lines, point (all year)

Mathematical Reasoning
continue a pattern of 5 objects,
alternate one property
complete puzzles of at least 10
pieces (all year)

compare groups of up to 4 objects
and use quantitative vocabulary

Orientation in Time and Space
time: today-tomorrow
time: use a weekly calendar to
locate day of the week (all year)
time: sequence and describe 3
images of events that have been
experienced at temporally
distinct times
space: next to-away from,
in front of-behind, up-down
space: river

Scientific Reasoning
describe objects using senses:
hearing

Music
produce sounds that are loud or
soft, long or short
vocally imitate isolated sounds
Instrumental Works: Bizet,
Overture from Carmen

Visual Arts
memory of visual details
printing (all year)
drawing (all year)
Colors: black, white

FEBRUARY
Movement
act out pantomime/charade
Game: Simon Says

Work Habits
work in orderly, persistent manner
(all year)
follow single-step oral directions
(all year)

Oral Language
ask or answer increasingly
elaborate questions (other than
those beginning with the 5
"W"s) (all year)

**Nursery Rhymes, Poems,
Fingerplays, Songs**
Rhymes: Did You Ever See a
Lassie?
Oh, Do You Know the Muffin
Man?

**Storybook Reading and
Storytelling**
sequence illustrations of 3 story
events (all year)
Stories: Ask Mr. Bear
Are You My Mother?

**Emerging Literacy Skills in
Reading and Writing**
dictate a caption for a photo or
drawing (all year)
writing strokes: spiral (all year)

Mathematical Reasoning
demonstrate 1-1 correspondence,
up to 4 objects
make a collection with the same
number of objects as another
collection, up to 4 objects

Orientation in Time and Space
time: identify by name – clock,
schedule, calendar
space: top-middle-bottom, under,
around
space: farm
space: reproduce parquetry or
mosaic design, placing objects
directly on design card

Scientific Reasoning
describe objects using senses:
touch

Music
indicate the number of sounds
heard
imitate clapping pattern sequences
of no more than 3 claps/pattern
imitate sequence of no more than 3
sounds/sequence
Instrumental Works: Offenbach,
"Can-can"

Visual Arts
fold, tape

MARCH
Movement
Game: Farmer in the Dell

Autonomy/Social Skills
follow rules for simple childhood
games (all year)

Oral Language
give simple single step directions
understand and use increasingly
elaborate imperatives

**Nursery Rhymes, Poems,
Fingerplays, Songs**
Rhymes: Oh Dear What Can the
Matter Be?
Eensy, Weensy Spider
Row, Row, Row Your Boat

**Storybook Reading and
Storytelling**
retell a story that has been read
aloud (all year)
Stories: The Little Red Hen
The Carrot Seed
Millions of Cats

**Emerging Literacy Skills in
Reading and Writing**
writing strokes: circle (all year)

Mathematical Reasoning
count groups of objects up to 4
(all year)
given an oral number, create
groups with the given number
of objects, up to 4 (all year)
identify and count pennies

Orientation in Time and Space
space: to the side-in the middle
space: situate oneself or objects in
space according to given spatial
terms
space: ocean

Scientific Reasoning
describe objects using senses:
smell

Music
accompany a story or musical
piece with previously taught
sound effects

Visual Arts
representational painting

APRIL
Movement
push a large, heavy object with
partner/group
Game: Hot Potato

Oral Language
combine simple sentences
    using "and"
use personal pronouns,
    especially "I"
match pictures of opposites

**Nursery Rhymes, Poems,
Fingerplays, Songs**
Rhymes: Hush Little Baby
    If You're Happy and You
        Know It
    Pop Goes the Weasel

**Storybook Reading and
Storytelling**
read/tell a story using a
    wordless picture book
Stories: A Boy, A Dog, A Frog
    Good Dog, Carl
    Goodnight Gorilla

**Emerging Literacy Skills in
Reading and Writing**
recognize the initial letter of
    one's name

Mathematical Reasoning
name and match numerals 1-4 with
    corresponding quantities
identify ordinal positions first/last
identify dollar bill

Orientation in Time and Space
space: indicate one's position on
    a simple room map
space: lake

Scientific Reasoning
select and use scissors to cut
    straight lines (all year)

Music
Instrumental Works: Ponchielli,
    "Dance of the Hours"

Visual Arts
cut

understand and use negative
    forms of sentences, questions
    and imperatives

**Nursery Rhymes, Poems,
Fingerplays, Songs**
Rhymes: Bingo
    The Wheels on the Bus
    Kookaburra

**Storybook Reading and
Storytelling**
identify previously read books
    by title and cover
Stories: Harold & the Purple
    Crayon
    Cat in the Hat
    The Runaway Bunny
    Chicka Chicka Boom Boom

**Emerging Literacy Skills in
Reading and Writing**
draw horizontal and vertical lines
    between two end points

Mathematical Reasoning
compare groups of numerals 1-4 to
    determine more than/greater
    than/less than
illustrate concept of "put together"
    and "take away" with up
    to 4 objects

Orientation in Time and Space
space: countryside

Music
move to music with a partner or
    group, performing simple
    movements
Visual Arts
representational drawing

MAY

Movement
Game: Mother May I

Oral Language
answer "what will happen if"
    questions

106

Level Two: **Month-by-Month Guide**

SEPTEMBER

Movement
relax specific body muscles and/or the whole body, from high activity level to quiet state
throw and kick object with increasing accuracy at a target (all year)
Game: Red Light, Green Light

Autonomy/Social Skills
draw a dimensional picture of a person (all year)
recognize, call by name and indicate role of school personnel

Work Habits
return toys and materials to their proper location (all year)

Oral Language
understand and use intonation and emphasis to ask a question, express surprise, agreement, displeasure, urgency (all year)
after listening to an oral description of a scene, recreate the scene in pictures (all year)
sequence and describe 3-5 images of events or phases of a single event that have been experienced (all year)

Nursery Rhymes, Poems, Fingerplays, Songs
memorize and recite independently a simple rhyme, poem, fingerplay or song (all year)
Rhymes: Who Stole the Cookie From the Cookie Jar?
Pledge of Allegiance
Doctor Foster
Ride a Cock Horse
Twinkle, Twinkle Little Star

Storybook Reading and Storytelling
attend and listen to picture books with storylines as well as nonfiction (all year)
sequence 5 illustrations of story events (all year)
Stories: The Town Mouse and the Country Mouse
Caps for Sale
Mike Mulligan & His Steam Shovel
The Park Bench

Emerging Literacy Skills in Reading and Writing
use a simplified, illustrated daily schedule of activities (all year)
read the first names of classmates (all year)
hold a writing instrument correctly (all year)
writing strokes: horizontal, vertical lines, spiral, circle (all year)

Mathematical Reasoning
identify pairs of objects/pictures as same or different
sort objects/pictures according to color, shape, size or function ("red/not red," "circle/not circle," "big/not big," "cooking utensil/not cooking utensil")
complete puzzles of at least 18 pieces (all year)
recite number sequence, 1-10 (all year)

Orientation in Time and Space
time: sequence chronologically and describe 3-5 images of events or phases of events that have been experienced (all year)
time: name the days of the week in sequence (all year)
time: name the days of the weekend
time: use a simple, illustrated schedule of daily activities to indicate which activity preceded and which will follow the current activity (all year)
space: in-on-outside, inside-outside, under-over
space: follow or give oral, spatially oriented directions to move from one location to another

Scientific Reasoning
identify body parts, including the following organs: heart, lungs
identify the body part and sense associated with certain sensations

Music
identify pairs of sounds as either the same or different
identify and associate sounds with the rhythm instruments that make them

Visual Arts
play games requiring matching of like images, such as domino games
collage (all year)
examine and create a work in the style of... Artwork: Matisse, The Snail (collage)
examine and talk about the details and story of... Artwork: Bearden, Summertime

OCTOBER

Movement
maintain balance on beam, walking forward, backward, sideways
navigate obstacle course using different movements (all year)
Game: Duck, Duck Goose

Autonomy/Social Skills
dress self independently (all year)
respect the personal belongings of others (all year)
interrupt a conversation politely (all year)

Oral Language
describe oneself, home and immediate family
carry on a conversation with another child (all year)

Nursery Rhymes, Poems, Fingerplays, Songs
Rhymes: Peter, Peter Pumpkin Eater

CONTINUED NEXT PAGE

I'm a Little Teapot
Oh Where, Oh Where Has
My Little Dog Gone?
This Is The Way the Ladies
Ride

**Storybook Reading and
Storytelling**
retell a story that has been read
aloud (all year)
Stories: Thumbelina
Frederick
Blueberries for Sal
A Child's Book of Great Art

**Emerging Literacy Skills in
Reading and Writing**
dictate a simple letter, invitation or
thank you note (all year)
writing strokes: moon, cross
(all year)
trace and then draw independently
outlines of geometric shapes,
irregular forms

Mathematical Reasoning
classify objects/pictures according
to color or shape
compare groups of objects of no
more than 6 objects/group and
use quantitative vocabulary to
describe them
demonstrate 1-1 correspondence
with concrete objects, up to and
including 6 objects
construct a collection of objects
having the same number as
another group, up to 6 objects

Orientation in Time and Space
time: name the current day of the
week, the day that was yesterday
and the day that will be
tomorrow (all year)
time: name and locate the day and
month on a calendar (all year)
time: use monthly calendar to
name holidays and special
events marked by symbols
(all year)
space: between, at the corner of,
above-below
space: trace the path described
on a picture map in which
different objects represent
different landmarks

Scientific Reasoning
care for, observe and record
observations of an animal
(all year)
select and use appropriate tool for
particular task: cut-scissors,
join paper-staple

Music
identify classmates by voice alone
imitate clapping pattern sequences
of at least 4 claps per pattern
that vary in tempo, number and
length of pauses between claps
(all year)

Visual Arts
use scissors and stapler as needed
in completing art projects
sculpture (all year)
examine and create a work in the
style of... Artwork: Egyptian,
Blue Hippo
examine and talk about the details
and story of... Artwork: Degas,
Little Fourteen Year Old Dancer

NOVEMBER

Movement
ride a tricycle (all year)
Game: Musical Chairs

Autonomy/Social Skills
ask appropriately for help (all year)
offer assistance to another child
(all year)

Work Habits
memorize address, phone number,
date of birth

Oral Language
identify and express physical
sensations, mental states,
emotional feelings using words
(all year)

**Nursery Rhymes, Poems,
Fingerplays, Songs**
interpret and act out through
pantomime a rhyme, poem or
fingerplay using one's own
gestures (all year)
Rhymes: Here We Go Round the
Mulberry Bush
At the Seaside

The Pancake
Do Your Ears Hang Low?
Jump or Jiggle

**Storybook Reading and
Storytelling**
predict events in a story (all year)
provide a new story ending
(all year)
Stories: How Turtle Flew South for
the Winter
The Story of Ferdinand
Strega Nona
Thanksgiving

**Emerging Literacy Skills in
Reading and Writing**
dictate a description to accompany
one's drawings of people,
objects, events or activities,
derived from experience or
imagination (all year)
follow a simple recipe (all year)
writing strokes: cane, hook (all year)

Mathematical Reasoning
classify objects/pictures according
to size, function or other
conceptual categories
identify and verbally label the
single common characteristic of
a group of objects/pictures
(all year)
identify and verbally label the differences or criteria used for the
classification of several groups
of objects/pictures (all year)
classify and name shapes as circles,
rectangles and triangles (all year)
count groups of objects with up to
6 objects (all year)
given an oral number, create
groups with the corresponding
number of objects (all year)

Orientation in Time and Space
time: name and locate date of birth
on monthly calendar
time: identify a horizontal series of
seven squares as representing
one week on a monthly calendar
space: toward, against, before-after
space: reproduce a pattern card
design using parquetry blocks,
mosaics or pegs
space: forest

Scientific Reasoning

identify and describe basic human
needs: food and drink, shelter
and protection from temperature
and weather

select and use appropriate tool for a
particular task: nail, join wood –
hammer

Music

use musical instruments or other
objects to imitate a sequence of 3
or more sounds made by more
than 1 instrument

listen to environmental sounds
presented as a sound story and
describe the events and context
in which they are occurring

Visual Arts

demonstrate memory of visual
details by playing
"Concentration" type of
memory games

demonstrate memory of colors
found in nature

painting (all year)

examine and create a work in the
style of... Artwork: Matisse, Red
Interior, Blue Table

DECEMBER

Movement

act out a nursery rhyme, poem,
fingerplay or other charade
(all year)

Game: Drop the Handkerchief

Autonomy/Social Skills

take turns using toys and sharing
materials (all year)

Work Habits

choose and use a toy or activity
independently for a sustained
period of time (all year)

Oral Language

describe an event or task that has
already taken place outside of
the immediate time and place
or that will take place

use present, past and future tenses

sort, classify and describe
objects/pictures according to
a conceptual category

Nursery Rhymes, Poems, Fingerplays, Songs

using familiar rhymes, poems, or
songs, finish a recitation with the
correct rhyming word

Rhymes: A Hunting We Will Go
Bat, Bat
The Old Woman Must Stand
At the Tub
One Misty, Moisty Morning

Storybook Reading and Storytelling

"read"/tell a story based on the
illustrations of a book with text
that has not been read
previously (all year)

Stories: The Little Engine That
Could
Sam and the Tigers
The Shoemaker and the Elves
"Eye Openers and
"Eyewitness Junior" books

Emerging Literacy Skills in Reading and Writing

associate spoken and written
language by matching written
word labels with spoken words
(all year)

segment a spoken sentence into
separate, distinct words

point to words as distinct units on
a page of print

writing strokes: bowl, bridge,
diagonal line (all year)

Mathematical Reasoning

select an object/picture according
to a description that includes
two properties

use a double entry table

find examples of circles and
rectangles in everyday objects

Orientation in Time and Space

time: sequence images depicting
the evolution and completion of
a project or undertaking over
an extended period of time

space: high-low, face to face - back
to back

space: copy a tower or construction
that has been made by another
person, using blocks of different
shapes, colors or sizes

space: mountain

Scientific Reasoning

observe, describe and record
some basic properties of water,
its presence and effects in the
world

select and use the appropriate tool
for a particular task: join fabric –
needle and thread

Music

accompany a story or musical
piece by introducing original
sound effects at the appropriate
moment

sing a round for 2 or more groups

Instrumental Works: Villa-Lobos,
The Little Train of Caipira
Herbert, March of the Toys
Strauss, Donner und Blitz

Visual Arts

use needle and thread to complete
an art project

drawing (all year)

examine and create a work in the
style of... Artwork: Miro, People
and Dog in Sun

work with other children to create
a collective work of art

JANUARY

Movement

play catch with a partner using
a large ball (all year)

Game: Kitty Wants A Corner

Autonomy/Social Skills

complete an activity or project
in conjunction with another
child or group (all year)

accept the consequences of
actions, positive and negative
(all year)

Oral Language

identify and name simple
opposites

assume a different role or
perspective and express
different possibilities,
imaginary or realistic
(all year)

CONTINUED NEXT PAGE

Nursery Rhymes, Poems, Fingerplays, Songs
Rhymes: January
   There Was a Fat Pig
   An Old Person from Ware
   Hickety, Pickety, My
      Black Hen
   One Potato, Two Potato

Storybook Reading and Storytelling
use cover and illustration clues to locate books that pertain to a particular topic or answer a question (all year)
Stories: Martin Luther King
   The Tale of Rabbit and Coyote
   Uncle Jed's Barbershop
   Why Flies Buzz in People's Ears
   "First Discovery" books

Emerging Literacy Skills in Reading and Writing
blend two parts of a compound word or two syllables (all year)
represent "in written form," following an actual experience: directions for completing a recipe or craft, scientific observations of experiments, events (all year)
writing strokes: wave, x, star, zigzag line (all year)
sing the ABC song

Mathematical Reasoning
continue a complex, 2-color pattern of objects as represented by a pattern card
create and verbally describe a pattern of concrete objects
divide an object into approximately equal pieces for 2 people
name and match the numerals 1-6 with the corresponding quantities

Orientation in Time and Space
time: use a year-long timeline to mark events (all year)
time: sequence and describe photos and/or drawings that represent a timeline of one's life and experiences
time: sequence photos and/or drawings of a baby, school-age child, young adult, elderly adult and describe in terms of the progression of the stages of development in the life of one person
space: match halves of symmetrical objects to make wholes
space: mark the location of specific objects, places on a simple map of a familiar location
space: jungle

Scientific Reasoning
sequence photos and/or drawings of a baby, school-age child, young adult and elderly adult to represent the life cycle

Music
move to music, individually interpreting and modifying one's movements, according to the tempo, intensity and rhythm
Instrumental Works: Mozart, Variations
   Debussy, Cakewalk
   Khachaturian, Sabre Dance

Visual Arts
painting (all year)
examine and create a work in the style of... Artwork: Delaunay, Rhythm
examine and talk about the details and story of... Artwork: Munier, Special Moment

FEBRUARY

Movement
complete a circuit or obstacle course, following arrows or path indicated (all year)

Autonomy/Social Skills
follow the rules for simple childhood games, circle games and board games (all year)

Work Habits
carry out multi step oral directions that have been accompanied by a preliminary demonstration (all year)

Oral Language
identify outcomes and possible causes (all year)
combine simple sentences using "but," "or" (all year)

Nursery Rhymes, Poems, Fingerplays, Songs
Rhymes: Singing Time
   Are You Sleeping?
   A Tisket, A Tasket
   Yankee Doodle
   Wee Willie Winkie

Storybook Reading and Storytelling
make up and tell a story (all year)
Stories: George Washington and the cherry tree
   Abe Lincoln and his humble origins
   Madeline
   Amazing Grace

Emerging Literacy Skills in Reading and Writing
given a sound and two words, identify the word that begins with the sound (all year)
assemble a simple object or craft following illustrated directions (all year)
write one's first name (all year)

Mathematical Reasoning
copy/represent and continue "on paper" an alternating pattern of 1 property or a 2-color pattern
compare pairs of objects and use comparative vocabulary to describe them: length, height, volume
name and write the numerals 1-6 in sequential order

Orientation in Time and Space
time: sequence photos and/or drawings of a baby, school-age child, young adult, elderly adult and describe in terms of generations in the context of one family
time: arrange photos and/or drawings of members of one's own family on genealogical tree or diagram
space: mark with arrows or other

symbols on a simple map the
path that has been taken from
one place to another (all year)
space: use the shortest route to go
from the exterior to the center
of a simple maze

Scientific Reasoning
classify images of animals
according to the habitat or
environment in which they
generally live: lake/river, ocean,
farm, forest (woods), jungle

Music
identify and associate sounds with
the instruments that make them
(piano, violin)
identify a selection of music as
either vocal or instrumental
maintain the beat of a chant, song

Visual Arts
printing (all year)
examine and create a work in the
style of... Artwork: Klee, Senecio
examine and talk about the details
and story of... Artwork: Hicks,
Noah's Ark

MARCH

Movement
carry a large object from 1 location
to another with a partner or
group

Autonomy/Social Skills
attempt to solve problems/conflicts
using words (all year)

Work Habits
describe and evaluate one's own
work, identify and correct
errors, refine work, with the
assistance and feedback of an
adult (all year)

Oral Language
carry on a simple conversation on
the phone
give simple, multi-step directions
understand and use sentences
with clauses: because, if, who,
that, when (all year)

Nursery Rhymes, Poems, Fingerplays, Songs
finish a recitation with a rhyming
word other than that of the
actual rhyme
Rhymes: Once I Saw a Little Bird
There Was a Crooked Man
The Worm
Raindrops
Five Little Ducks That I Once
Knew

Storybook Reading and Storytelling
attend and listen to books with
minimal or no illustrations
(all year)
point to words that begin with
same letter as own name
Stories: Bobo's Magic Wishes
The Littles
Tikki Tikki Tembo

Emerging Literacy Skills in Reading and Writing
use a simplified, illustrated
telephone listing
give the beginning sound of a word
(all year)
identify the name and sound of the
letters in one's name (all year)

Mathematical Reasoning
compare pairs of objects and use
comparative vocabulary to
describe them: size, mass,
temperature
use an arbitrary tool of
measurement to compare the
length and height of objects
organize and read quantitative data
in simple bar graphs
identify and count pennies up
to six

Orientation in Time and Space
time: mark events across several
generations with a century
timeline
time: consider photos/drawings of
activities associated with specific
periods of life in reference to his
present age and indicate
whether these activities are part
of his past, present or future
experiences

space: color squares on a blank
grid to reproduce designs on
other grids
space: continue a linear frieze-like
pattern of symbols on a grid
space: island

Scientific Reasoning
observe, describe and record
some basic properties of light,
its presence and effects in the
physical world
plant, care for, observe and
record observations of a plant
(all year)
select and use the appropriate tool
to complete a particular task:
dig a hole/trowel, shovel; water
a plant/watering can, hose

Music
Instrumental Works: Schumann,
Dreams

Visual Arts
examine and create a work in the
style of... Artwork: Mondrian,
Broadway Boogie-Woogie
examine the details and tell the
story of... Artwork: Rousseau,
The Sleeping Gypsy
describe one's own artwork,
explaining the materials and
techniques used (all year)

APRIL

Movement
maintain momentum on a swing
by pumping legs
Game: Relay Races

Work Habits
organize and plan what is needed
to carry out a project or task,
with adult assistance when
needed (all year)

Oral Language
give a detailed, sequential
explanation of how to do
something so that the activity
can be carried out by another
person
understand and use sentences
with clauses: before, after,
while, as soon as (all year)

Nursery Rhymes, Poems, Fingerplays, Songs
Rhymes: Tom, Tom the Piper's Son
Five Little Monkeys
John Jacob Jingleheimer
Schmidt
Looby Loo
Blue Tail Fly

Storybook Reading and Storytelling
demonstrate book and print
awareness
Stories: My Father's Dragon
Mufaro's Beautiful Daughters
Where the Wild Things Are

Emerging Literacy Skills in Reading and Writing
begin to use invented phonetic
spelling in writing (all year)
indicate the number of phonemes
(1 – 3) heard in a real or
nonsense word (all year)

Mathematical Reasoning
use a ruler to compare the
length and height of objects
play a simple game using a die
to move the number of spaces
shown
compare pairs of numerals, 1-6,
using more/greater than or
less than
identify by name a quarter
illustrate the concept of "put
together" and "take away" with
groups of 1-6 objects (all year)
label the action of "put together" as
adding and "take away" as
subtracting (all year)

Orientation in Time and Space
time: match images of
contemporary objects with like
objects from the past, indicating
whether they belong to, the past
or present
space: use simple coordinates to
locate a point on a grid
space: name city, state and country
in which she lives
space: locate own state on U. S.
map
space: city

Scientific Reasoning
observe some basic properties of
air, its presence and effects in
the physical world

Music
move to music using a sequence
of choreographed steps or
movements to music

Visual Arts
examine the details and tell the
story of... Artwork: Johnson,
The Old Stagecoach

MAY

Movement
Game: Tag

Oral Language
express a personal opinion
understand and use complex
sentences with clauses:
so that, (verb)+ing

Nursery Rhymes, Poems, Fingerplays, Songs
Rhymes: I Know An Old Lady
Oats Peas Beans and Barley
Grow
Teddy Bears' Picnic
You Are My Sunshine

Storybook Reading and Storytelling
Stories: Betsy Ross and the Flag
Children Just Like Me
Miss Rumphius
People

Emerging Literacy Skills in Reading and Writing
give the beginning sound of a
spoken word

Mathematical Reasoning
seriate at least 3 items by length,
height or size
add and subtract problems
represented by numerals 1-4,
using objects or pictures as
needed
indicate that a dollar bill has
more value than a penny or
quarter

Orientation in Time and Space
time: distinguish objects of the
more recent past from the
more distant past
space: left-right
space: on U. S. map and globe,
identify land and ocean areas

Scientific Reasoning
create or construct a project

Visual Arts
examine the details and tell the
story of... Artwork: Pippin,
The Domino Players

Organizing
and
Integrating:
The Preschool
Sequence
and Daily
Scheduling

Organizing and Integrating: **The Preschool Sequence and Daily Scheduling**

As noted throughout this document, the Core Knowledge Preschool Sequence specifies what to teach, not how to teach. The following suggestions, however, are offered to encourage teachers to make use of a wide variety of organizational possibilities.

Some of the competencies by their nature lend themselves to particular organizational strategies in terms of the types of experiences provided. For example, the competencies that focus on using appropriate social skills will be most naturally addressed in group settings. Conversely, development of the emerging literacy competency of associating sounds with the written letters of one's own name might be best approached individually.

By and large, however, most of the Preschool Sequence competencies can, and should, be presented in a variety of ways. These may include large – or small – group activities; one-on-one teacher-child or one-on-one peer interaction; child initiated or "free play" center activities; center activities structured by the materials provided; selection of the center for the child by the teacher; and so on.

The manner in which a variety of organizational strategies may be used can be illustrated by considering a specific example from the Preschool Sequence, the patterning competencies in the math section. The teacher might first introduce and demonstrate the concept of patterning in a large group. Later, he or she might work with a small group of children, making patterns together, while the remainder of the children participate in free play center activities. At another time, the teacher might take aside and work with just one child, in order to scaffold learning, challenging, but not frustrating, the child, one step at a time. At yet another time, he or she might pair together two students, one who is skillful at patterning and one who is not, asking the more competent student to create patterns for the other to copy. The teacher might also create a center with a variety of materials that lend

themselves to pattern making – unifix blocks, small manipulative objects of different colors and sizes, paper, stickers, colored markers, colored paper strips to make into paper chains, etc. Children visiting the center would be encouraged to create their own patterns. (Sample patterning activities further illustrating the manner in which different organizational strategies may be used to reinforce the same concept follow on the next page).

The possibility of so many organizational strategies for presenting experiences permits each teacher to creatively personalize the Preschool Sequence to best meet the needs of the children in his or her class. For teachers not accustomed to considering a full range of organizational strategies, the initial selection and management of these possibilities may present new challenges. Teachers are encouraged to consciously avoid an either-or approach, for example, using only "free play" center type activities or only large group activities. As they become increasingly familiar with both the Preschool Sequence and their own students' particular needs, teachers will more easily and effectively integrate a variety of organizational strategies in their daily activities.

Sample
Patterning
Activities
and
Organizational
Strategies

Sample Patterning Activities and Organizational Strategies

Circle time, whole group

Monday: Clapping patterns, fast/slow, loud/soft.
Tuesday: Introduce pattern shelf paper, have children show the patterns.
Wednesday: Pattern in the weather symbols, sunny/cold, sunny/cold, sunny/cold.
Thursday: Song with a pattern of movement.
Friday: Highlight patterns children are wearing, have them tell about the patterns.

Snack time, whole group

Monday: cereal and raisins
Tuesday: popcorn and cheese squares
Wednesday: goldfish and pretzels
Thursday: peanuts and sunflower seeds in the shells
Friday: blueberries and grapes

Transition, lining up for recess

Monday: Line up boy/girl/boy/girl
Tuesday: Line up standing/sitting/standing/sitting
Wednesday: Line up boy standing/girl sitting/boy standing/girl sitting
Thursday: Children line themselves up in a pattern
Friday: Children line themselves up in a pattern

Small group time

Monday: Given two groups of five unifix cubes of different colors, children will watch a demonstration, and then put their cubes into a ABAB pattern. Some will be challenged to make a different kind of pattern.

Tuesday: Given pattern cards and beads, children will follow the pattern on the card by stringing beads. The other group will be given two shades of brown wood beads, light and dark, and will make a ABAB pattern or another of their choice, by stringing beads on a plastic lanyard. They will take these necklaces home. Groups will switch activities half way through.

Wednesday: Given two triangles, children will glue them together to make a star of David, and check their work by saying point/space/point/space as they touch the points and spaces around the star. They will then use glue and glitter to decorate them.

Thursday: Given a paper with two candy canes drawn on it, the children will use crayon or marker to make a ABAB pattern. They then cut them apart, some to take home, and some to decorate the school room with.

Friday: Friday's activity requires that strips of green, red and white paper be sent home with children earlier in the week. With their parent's help, children write their holiday traditions on the strips. In school, the children use the strips to make paper chains of the colors in patterns they choose.

The sample activities were developed and used in the field test class by Catherine Howanstine at St. Leonard's Elementary School, Calvert County, Maryland.

Regardless of whether a half-day or full-day is implemented, a minimum of $2\frac{1}{2}$ hours of constructive learning time is recommended.

The Preschool Sequence may be implemented in either half or full day settings. The daily schedules and commentary below, are presented as just one possibility for each setting.[1]

SAMPLE HALF-DAY SCHEDULE

8:45 - 9:15	Arrival
9:15 - 9:40	Large Group Time/ Opening Exercises
9:40 - 9:45	Planning
9:45 - 10:30	Center Time
10:30 - 10:40	Clean-Up
10:45 - 10:55	Snack/Review
10:55 - 11:15	Outdoor Play
11:15 - 11:35	Tub Time or Small Group Time
11:35 - 11:45	Story time
11:45 - 11:55	Dismissal

SAMPLE FULL DAY SCHEDULE

7:30 - 8:00	Arrival
8:00 - 8:30	Large Group Time/ Opening Exercises
8:30 - 8:50	Breakfast
8:50 - 9:15	Tub Time
9:15 - 9:30	Small Group Time
9:30 - 9:35	Planning
9:35 - 10:35	Center Time
10:35 - 10:50	Clean Up
10:50 - 11:00	Snack
11:00 - 11:30	Outdoor Play
11:30 - 11:50	Large Group Time
11:50 - 12:15	Lunch
12:15 - 12:30	Story Time
12:30 - 1:30	Rest Time
1:30 - 1:45	Daily Review/ Share Time
1:45 - 2:00	Dismissal

NOTES

ARRIVAL:

- Hang up coat, book bag, check for notes
- Look for name card and place on daily attendance chart
- Select job for the day on job chart
- Journal writing - write or draw; ask teacher/aide to write the date or any other captions, comments
- Find a table toy or book to use at the table
- Cleanup at signal

LARGE GROUP – OPENING EXERCISES:

- Come to circle, find name card, sit in that space
- Pledge of Allegiance
- Office Announcements
- Review of Daily Attendance Chart - who's here, who's missing, read name cards
- Review of Daily Job Chart
- Calendar and Weather Activities
- Songs/Nursery Rhymes/ Fingerplays
- Recap of what was done yesterday, what will be done today, presentation of what's new in centers, etc.
- Increase the length of large group time gradually: at the start of the year, include fewer activities and meet for shorter time.

PLANNING:

- Children tell what they will do in the center that either they have chosen or that the teacher has chosen for them; teacher briefly notes each child's plan on dry erase or blackboard. As children gain planning skill, they work in pairs, taking turns assuming the role of the teacher, asking for the other's plan.

CENTER TIME:

- Center pockets and name cards can be used to manage how many children may participate in a center. At the start of year, each center has the same number of pockets as children that may use the center; children place 1 name card per

pocket. Later in the year, centers can each have a single pocket, with dots on the outside of the pocket, indicating how many children may use the center. Children count the dots, count name cards already in the pocket and place their name card in the pocket only if there is room.
- Introduce limited number of centers at the start of the year; always model and talk about possible use of each new center. Gradually add other centers. As the year progresses, periodically add new materials to existing centers or replace some centers with completely new centers.
- Clean up at signal; always provide "advance warning"; return all items to their proper classroom location.

TUB TIME:

- Tub = plastic, Tupperware-style tub containing 1 game or set of educational materials that children are capable of using independently. Examples of items that may be included in a tub: linear pattern cards and manipulatives; sorting cups and manipulatives; geoboards, rubber bands and shape cards; parquetry blocks and patterns; unifix cubes; dominoes; lotto game; listening game lotto with cassette; story sequence cards; sticker scene sets, rhyming objects or cards etc.
- Placemats or small trays placed with each tub indicate how many children may use each tub. Tub lids can be color coded, i.e., red = math activities, blue = language activities, etc. Teacher may assign each child to a color category, if desired, allowing child to pick particular tub.
- Follow same introduction and cleanup suggestions made for centers (above).

SMALL GROUP TIME:

- Use for a variety of activities, including science experiments, art activities, cooking, language experience stories.
- Use to reinforce a particular

competency with those children who are having difficulty or need more practice.

• Keep small groups flexible: group children on any given day according to needs, interests.

SNACK:

• If school provides snack, menu can be written on dry erase or blackboard using numerals, rebuses and words. Place snack items in baskets; children take designated number of each item. They may help each other count as they take 6 grapes, for example.

• Use this time to review what children did during the morning; check correspondence with their original written plans, etc.

OUTDOOR PLAY:

• Include time for both free play and exploration and more structured movement activities, organized group games.

• Provide materials for climbing, throwing, etc; create "obstacle courses."

STORY TIME:

• Vary the organizational strategies used during story time: large group, small group (books rotated between groups over several days), etc.

• Use this time to review stories read the previous day, to act out or retell story, etc.

• Later in the year, introduce "DEAR" (Drop Everything and Read): everyone, including the teacher, chooses something to read.

LARGE GROUP TIME:

• Use for music and movement activities, story time.

• Increase the length of large group time gradually: at the start of the year, require shorter period of "listening time."

BREAKFAST, LUNCH:

• If school provides meal, menu can be written on dry erase or blackboard using numerals, rebuses and words; refer to menu in serving foods.

• Use this time to teach social skills at mealtime, conversational skills, etc.

DISMISSAL/DAILY REVIEW:

• Review activities during the day, what was done when during the day, what children liked best, etc.; incorporate reference to daily schedule, calendar.

OTHER HINTS AND NOTES:

• **Plan for transition times between activities: provide advance warnings before changes; use signals, such as a cleanup song, timer, etc.; whenever possible, make "waiting time" (while other children finish cleanup, get in line, etc.) enjoyable, worthwhile - sing a song, play "I Spy," "Twenty Questions,"etc.**

• **Be sure to visually represent and display daily schedule in images and words; refer to frequently throughout the day - "What are we going to do next?," "What did we do after lunch?," etc.**

• **Recognize that you cannot touch on every area of the Preschool Sequence every day. Strive for a weekly balance.**

Scaffolding
Learning:
Guiding
Young
Children to
Increasing
Competency

Scaffolding Learning: Guiding Young Children to Increasing Competency

Once again, it is important to note that the Core Knowledge Preschool Sequence specifies what to teach, not how to teach. Some comment on methodology, however, is appropriate as, in recent years, many American early childhood professionals have been led to believe that the kind of stimulating material presented in the Preschool Sequence is inappropriate for young children.

Prevailing thought and practice in American preschools during the past decade, derived largely from Piagetian theory, has been characterized by a predominant reliance upon child-initiated learning as the primary, if not sole, means of cognitive development and knowledge acquisition. In recent years, both cognitive research, as well as exposure to international early childhood practices, have led to a more balanced view of child development. There is increased awareness of the importance of the sociocultural context for cognitive development and knowledge acquisition. While the active participation of the child is essential to the construction of knowledge, it is now recognized that this process does not occur in a vacuum: the social environment serves as the support system that allows the child to move forward and continue to build new competencies with ever increasing autonomy. This new understanding of child development has important implications for the approach taken in preschool classes.

It is now understood that teachers, as well as parents, older peers, and so on, are active participants, not passive facilitators, in leading children to ever increasing levels of competence. Content knowledge and skills that may have been perceived as inappropriate for young children to discover on their own, are now seen as accessible through the intermediary of competent individuals in the child's social environment who bridge the gap between the child's existing knowledge and skills and those toward which he is striving.

The Preschool Sequence designates specific knowledge and skills. Using these competencies as end goals, teachers are able to start wherever the child is and identify intermediate steps, activities and strategies that will, with practice, lead to the final goal. This collaborative process between teacher and learner has been referred to in the educational literature as scaffolding, with the teacher initially providing much support and direction for the novice learner, gradually decreasing assistance as the child gains greater skill. In this way, the child's current skills and knowledge always become the starting place for new experiences and instruction, rather than a limitation or restriction.

THE KEY TO SCAFFOLDING is to structure a task so that it is challenging for the child, slightly above his or her independent level of functioning, but not frustrating. This may be accomplished by modifying several variables in the learning environment.

First, the teacher may modify and structure the task itself in such a way that what was difficult and out of reach falls more readily within the child's grasp. This may be achieved by breaking down a skill, for example, into smaller components. To do this, the teacher would begin by reflecting upon the end goal and then list, sequentially, each thing that one must do in order to successfully accomplish this goal. Often times, it may be helpful for the teacher to actually physically perform the task him- or herself, while making note of each subskill or step that is required to do so.

The teacher would then offer experiences and activities designed to provide practice in each new step of the task. These individual steps may be made easier or more difficult by:

- varying the nature of the materials used: concrete, manipulative materials are more immediately understood than abstract, symbolic representations. For example, a child just beginning to create patterns will experience greater success in pattern making by first using 3-D objects and then moving to more symbolic representations, photos, drawings or verbal descriptions.
- modifying the similarities or differences between "correct" and "incorrect" responses. For example, a child just beginning to differentiate and sort shapes faces an easier, more manageable task if initially presented with circles and squares to sort, instead of circles and ovals.
- providing or eliminating cues that suggest the "correct answer." For example, the correct answer may be depicted as larger or in a different color than the other choices. Once the child is successful in selecting the correct response with these prompts, they are gradually eliminated.
- limiting or expanding the number of possible choices of answers or actions. It may be easier to first ask the child to sort circles and squares, instead of circles, squares, rectangles and triangles.
- asking a child to demonstrate receptive understanding or to

117

actually produce a response on his own. Matching activities are generally easier than those that require an independent response from the child. For example, it will be easier for a child just learning colors to respond first to, "Here's a red block. Show me the other blocks that look red like this one," later to, "Show me all the red blocks," and finally to, "What color is this?"

In addition, teachers can vary the degree of assistance that they offer, initially providing a high degree of more directed assistance for novice learners. The degree of assistance may be modified by:

• whether or not a model is provided and how complete or detailed the model is. For example, for a child just learning to tie his shoes, the teacher might initially perform all the steps in the tying process, leaving just the last step, tightening the bow, for the child to complete. Subsequently, the teacher might begin the tying process, but perform fewer and fewer steps herself, moving the child progressively closer to independent tying.

• the immediacy and frequency of feedback and error correction. When a teacher is seated next to a child, making comments simultaneously as he performs a task, she is providing a greater degree of structured assistance and support than if she asks the child to attempt the entire task on his own and then show it to her for feedback.

• the degree of specificity in the teacher's comments or questions. For example, open-ended comments or questions, such as "What do you think we should try next?" are less directive than more explicit questions, such as, "Do you think we should try the blue or red piece next?"

Said another way —

"Teachers are those who use themselves as bridges, over which they invite their students to cross; then having facilitated their crossing, joyfully collapse, encouraging them to create bridges of their own."

—Nikos Kazantzakis

Language of
Instruction:
How to
Incorporate
Into Daily
Lessons

**FOR ADDITIONAL
INFORMATION:**
See "Language of
Instruction" in the Preschool
Sequence Introduction and
following each section of the
Preschool Sequence.

Language of Instruction: **How to Incorporate Into Daily Lessons**

Teachers implementing the Core Knowledge Preschool Sequence should focus particular attention on incorporating the Language of Instruction in all classroom activities. In using this precise, content related vocabulary in their own speech, teachers provide preschoolers with the language and knowledge base that they will need to profit from formal academic instruction in elementary school.

Each discipline of the Preschool Sequence includes a Language of Instruction subsection with suggested lists of vocabulary words. The intent is that teachers use these words in their own speech as they interact and talk with children. However, do note that within each Language of Instruction section, the vocabulary words are presented in two categories:

Teacher Only

Specific words intended for use by the teacher; the goal is exposure to school talk. Most preschool children will not, as yet, spontaneously use these same words in their own speech, although some may, given appropriate, repeated pairings of experience and language.

Teacher and Children

Specific words that the teacher should use in her own speech and which are also reasonable to expect preschoolers to use. These vocabulary words are cited in the student goals of each discipline, but are repeated in the Language of Instruction to prompt the teacher to use this vocabulary in her own speech.

The word lists included in the Preschool Sequence are but a starting point. For any given activity, teachers should also brainstorm additional vocabulary words that might be meaningfully introduced in the context of the activity. Multi-syllable words that might typically be considered outside preschoolers' vocabularies should also be included, not excluded. Research has suggested that it is precisely this kind of adult use of occasional "rare words" that enriches children's own language skills.

In order to be sure that they include the Language of Instruction in their day-to-day activities, many teachers make a note of the vocabulary words in their lesson plans. Others write or post the words they want to focus on during a particular day or week on a blackboard, bulletin board or chart tablet as a highly visible reminder.

Teachers should use the vocabulary from the Language of Instruction while presenting information, describing something that he or she is demonstrating or describing what the children are doing. It is most effective to use the vocabulary word in a sentence and then rephrase the sentence, substituting a familiar word or group of words for the new vocabulary. When possible, it is also effective to show an illustration or object to clarify the meaning.

Here are several examples illustrating how teachers can meaningfully incorporate new vocabulary into their discussions with young children. The vocabulary word from the Language of Instruction is in italics:

"I wonder if the salt is going to *dissolve* when we put it in the water.... When something *dissolves* in water, it means that it mixes in completely with the water so that we don't see it any more at the bottom of the glass. It disappears. What do you think? Do you think that this salt is going to *dissolve* in the water so we won't see the salt anymore?"

"Let's check the *temperature* outside. The *temperature* tells us how hot or how cold it is."

"Can you *pantomime* this rhyme? When we *pantomime* a rhyme, we act it out, like this.... ."

"Please *apologize* to Brent. When you *apologize* to someone, you say you are sorry."

119

Zip to Zowie!
Math
Exploration
in a Pre-
Kindergarten
Classroom

NOTE:

See www.coreknowledge.org
for other sample preschool
lessons.

*see RESOURCE A:
A resource list of school supply
catalogs that carry these items

Zip to Zowie! Math Exploration
in a Pre-Kindergarten Classroom

Following are sample lessons, intended to span four weeks, created by Debbie Riley, of the Pre-Kindergarten/Head Start program at Three Oaks Elementary School in Fort Myers, Florida.

The goal is to create a classroom environment that promotes and develops math concepts in a pre-kindergarten classroom. This unit focuses on the development of centers that foster exploration and mastery of sorting and classification, patterning, and simple measurement.

PRESCHOOL SEQUENCE GOALS

MATHEMATICAL REASONING AND NUMBER SENSE

- Sort and classify objects or pictures of objects
- Duplicate and continue linear patterns
- Perceive and recognize shapes
- Use simple measurement and arrange objects in a series.

3-4 years
- Identify identical/different pairs varying in large detail, by one attribute, or group association
- Sort objects/pictures by a single attribute: color or shape

4-5 years
- Identify identical/different pairs varying in minor detail
- Sort objects/pictures by a single attribute: size or function
- Orally identify/label the criteria used to classify objects in a group
- Sort objects/pictures according to two characteristics

- Fill in the boxes of vertical and horizontal rows with objects using two criteria

3-4 years
- Duplicate a 1:1 pattern with 6 - 10 objects
- Match objects arranged in a pattern

4-5 years
- Create a more complex pattern with a pattern card [2:2 or 2:1:2]
- Using stickers or markers, continue an alternating pattern of one attribute– color, size, shape, or a two color pattern
- Create and orally describe a pattern using concrete objects

3-4 years
- Complete puzzles with ten or more interlocking pieces
- Match rectanglular, square, circular, and triangular shapes to their respective outlines
- Classify and name a circle

4-5 years:
- Classify and name a rectangle, triangle
- Determine geometric shapes in everyday objects
- Divide an object into two pieces of relatively equal sizes
- Examine pairs of objects using these terms:
    length: long/short
    volume: full/empty
    mass: heavy/light
    temperature: hot/cold
    size: large/small,
        thick/thin,
        wide/narrow
    height: tall/short
- Compare objects using non-standard units of measure [blocks, hands]:
    length:taller/shorter
    height:taller/shorter

- Rank and order at least three items in a series by length, height, or size using descriptive terms:
    length:longest/shortest
    height:tallest/shortest
    size: largest/smallest

BACKGROUND

READING
Mathematics Their Way
    Baratta-Lorton, Mary
    Menlo Park, CA
    Addison-Wesley, 1979

Explorations for Early Childhood
    Harcourt, Lalie
    Don Mills, Ontario
    Addison-Wesley, 1988

RESOURCES*
Manipulatives:
colored blocks, pattern blocks, unifix cubes, collections of animals, counting chips, coins, links, transportation vehicles, attribute shapes, geoboards and geobands, buttons, magnetic shapes, flannel board shapes, lacing beads, assorted groups of picture cards
Pattern cards:
for each group of manipulatives
Storage containers:
for the manipulatives
Assorted recording materials:
individually sized chalk boards and dry erase boards, clipboards, paper, rubber stamps and colored ink pads, crayons, dry erase markers, colored markers, pens, pencils, rulers

*see Resource B: model and directions for making this graph, see also:

Resource C: Who is here today? label

TEACHERS: Lessons occur during transitions, small group, and large group settings.

Independent practice occurs during "tubbing" and center times.

MATH CONCEPT I:

Sort and classify objects or pictures of objects

MATERIALS

- laminated construction paper, tongue depressors, shape patterns
- eight labeled storage containers, each filled with manipulatives to serve up to four children
- four workmats for each tub [easily made by laminating 2 sheets of 12" x 18" construction paper and then cutting the sheets in half to make 4 workmats]
- labels for the storage tubs, workmats, and area of the classroom where the manipulatives will be used
- three circular mats, rings, or trays for sorting objects during large group time [hula hoops work well]
- posterboard divided into 6 rows and 5 columns, 3" x 5" name cards for each student, 1" self-stick velcro tabs, one 3" x 5" construction paper shape of each color: red, yellow, green, blue, and orange

PRIOR KNOWLEDGE FOR STUDENTS

- Determine the prior knowledge students possess once procedures for working with manipulatives in the classroom have been taught at the beginning of the year. Allow children to explore the objects during a set time each day. Use this time daily to observe at what levels the children interact with the materials to determine a baseline for their functioning level. These initial assessments provide the basis for instruction.

KEY VOCABULARY

- same, alike, different, matching, group, property

PROCEDURES/ACTIVITIES

Environment I

- Prepare the classroom before children begin the school year by labeling each child's storage space and/or workbasket with a colored geometric shape. For twenty children, one each of a heart, circle, triangle, and square was made in orange, blue, green, yellow, and red. Upon entering class, each child chooses a shape he/she likes and that becomes his/her "symbol" for the year.
- Prepare job sticks and sleeping mats in the same way: using each child's symbol to identify job helpers and mats.
- Label areas in the classroom where children will work with the manipulatives as well as a place for storage when not in use. Label each of four sides of the "tub" container with the same color symbol used to label the room. Four workmats, also of the same color, should be made and available for each tub. The workmats define working space as well as number of children allowed to work at an individual tub.
- Refer to the shapes many times throughout the ensuing days- "Whose cubbie is the green triangle?" "Yellow circle is feeding the rabbit today." "Who is the yellow circle?"

Transitions/Large Group I

- "Matching Games" Distribute a colored block [red, yellow or blue] to each child as he/she sits in a circle for large group time.
- Place large rings in the center of the circle for matching each color.
- The teacher begins by placing a colored block in the center of one ring.
- Each child takes a turn placing his/her block in a ring, determining where it belongs and why. Elicit vocabulary from children as they place their blocks in the ring-same, different, color name, etc. This game can be played again and again and made more or less chal-

lenging by substituting different objects and matching color, size, shape, thickness, function, or group association.

Tubbing I

- Children then practice this "matching" concept in groups and individually at the tubs.
- Teachers extend and develop concepts during learning conversations with a child while he/she is working at a tub. For example, if matching groups are made, ask the child for the distinguishing characteristic.
- Contents of tubs are exchanged for more challenging materials as the children's skill level increases, for example, assorted sizes of red buttons are sorted by numbers of holes.

Environment II

- Make a "Who is here today?" chart * on poster board drawing five rows and six columns. Trace a circle, a heart, a square and a rectangle along the bottom row to represent the horizontal, or "x" axis. Use red, yellow, green, blue and orange pieces of paper to represent the vertical, or "y" axis. Then make name cards for each of the students by gluing their symbol onto the card. Laminate both the graph and name cards.

Transitions/Large Group II

- "Who is here today?" Introduce the children to name tags during morning circle time (for example, while taking attendance) first using symbols, then name and symbol, and later name only.
- "Sorting Activities" The cards may be sorted on the floor by color, shape, by beginning letters of the children's names, etc.
- Model placing the name cards on the chart "Who is here today?" At first, only use the color "x" axis as a guide for placing the cards on the chart. Let the children begin placing their name cards on the row of the color of their symbol

each morning. When the matching concept is grasped, play a switching game: cover up the colors and have the children place their name cards on the row with their symbol shape. Finally, let the students place their name card on the chart using both criteria, color and symbol.

Tubbing II

* see Appendix D: work mat grid

• Add new tubs or replace little used manipulatives with objects that could be sorted in two ways (for example, color/shape, animals/number of legs) and create large grid construction paper workmats.*
• Children practice sorting, using two attributes, at these tubs.
• Teachers assist, listen, and observe as children explain the criteria they have used to graph the tubbing materials.
• Evaluation/Assessment
concrete: observations during work with manipulatives, observations of transfer throughout the day, photographs, models
pictorial: matching objects to pattern cards
abstract: recording the matching objects on paper

MATH CONCEPT II:

Duplicate And Continue Linear Patterns

MATERIALS

• balloons, calendar shapes reflecting colors or patterns
• art print- "Rhythm" Sonia Delaunay
• Eight labeled storage containers, each filled with manipulatives to serve up to four children plus four workmats for each tub
• 2" x 18" construction paper or tagboard strips

PRIOR KNOWLEDGE FOR STUDENTS

• Explore and describe similarities and differences and attributes of things.
• Sort and match by one attribute.
• Determine the prior knowledge students possess once procedures for working with manipulatives have been taught at the beginning of the year. Allow children to explore the objects during a set time each day. Use this time daily to observe at what levels the children interact with the materials to determine a baseline for their functioning level. These initial assessments provide the basis for instruction.

KEY VOCABULARY

• repeating, pattern, continue the pattern, extend the pattern

PROCEDURES/ACTIVITIES

Environment I

• At the beginning of the year, set up a "Days of the Week" bulletin board that includes a balloon hanging below each school day name each week. The balloons are arranged in a 1:1 color pattern at the beginning of the year. Later in the year, the patterns can be made more challenging [e.g: alternating shapes, 2:1:2].

Large Group I

• Beginning on the first day of school, hang balloons for every day

of that week beneath the day label, creating a visual pattern for the children. Prior to popping a balloon to signify the day, repeat the colors of the pattern that the balloons have made.
• Repeat the color pattern of the balloons daily. After the last balloon color has been stated, begin to ask the children to guess which color would extend the pattern. [Later change the balloon shapes to create a new type of pattern.]

Environment II

• Each day, a student holds a miniature American flag during the Pledge of Allegiance. Since it is a popular responsibility, children notice the bright red and white stripe pattern the flag possesses.

Transition/Large Group II

• Regularly point out patterns in children's clothing, and create patterns through music, clapping, children lining up, etc.
• During large group, introduce the American flag and point out the red and white stripe pattern.
• Model patterning for the children by recreating the flag's striped pattern on lined paper with their assistance.

Tubbing I

• Introduce new ways to interact with tubbing materials during large group, small group, or transition time. Adding links and lacing beads is popular with the children for patterning.
• During tubbing, the children may create and extend patterns of their own choosing.

Center Activities

• home living: beading, jewelry making, weaving, quilting
• office center: stamps and ink pads, stickers
• blocks: post and lentil style architecture
• woodworking: nail patterns
• science: magnetic shape patterns
• writing: paper, dry erase boards,

clip boards and paper as well as writing utensils
- art: clay, mosaics, collage materials [also painting and drawing; see Environment 3]

Environment III

- Display the art print "Rhythm" by Sonia Delaunay.

Transition/Large Group III

- Introduce the art print "Rhythm" during large group. Have the children examine it to see if they can determine any patterns in her art work. [eg: colors, wide/narrow lines]
- The children then may suggest how they would create a painting or drawing in the style of Delaunay, using repeating patterns. Each individual may choose the medium.

Tubbing II

- Encourage the children to begin creating or replicating patterns on paper using shapes, colors, letters, etc. Then have them restate how they created the pattern they made.

Evaluation/Assessment

- **concrete:** observations during work with manipulatives, observations of transfer throughout the day, photographs, models
- **pictorial:** matching objects to pattern cards
- **abstract:** drawing or creating a pattern on paper, chalk board, or dry erase board

MATH CONCEPT III:

Use Simple Measurement Skills and Seriate Objects

MATERIALS

- yarn
- butcher paper, marker, crayons
- Cuisenaire Rods
- measuring cups, spoons
- balance
- cutting board, sharp knife

PRIOR KNOWLEDGE FOR STUDENTS

- Explore and describe similarities and differences of things.
- Determine the prior knowledge students possess once procedures for working with manipulatives have been taught at the beginning of the year. Allow children to explore the objects during a set time each day. Use this time daily to observe at what levels the children interact with the materials to determine a baseline for their functioning level. These initial assessments provide the basis for instruction.

KEY VOCABULARY

- short/tall (er) (est)
- short/long (er) (est)
- heavy (ier) (iest), measure

PROCEDURES/ACTIVITIES

Environment I

- Label groups of increasing/decreasing sized objects from largest to smallest or the reverse for daily storage, for example, pots and pans, measuring cups, measuring spoons, water table buckets.

Transition/Large Group/ Small Group I

- Introduce stacking bowls, nesting cups, or stacking rings to the children.
- Begin with only three of any group and determine the largest, smallest, and middle sized objects.

Tubbing I

- Add items to tubbing materials that can be ordered by size, weight, or color intensity.
- Students practice, through trial and error, to determine the relative order of the tubbing objects.

Environment II

- Daily, measure the outside temperature with red construction paper strips held against a classroom thermometer for guidance. Keep track of the temperature daily to determine patterns. The longer the red strip, the warmer the weather is, and vice versa.
- Also place a growth chart in the classroom as well as a large tape measure to pique children's interest in measuring their height.

Transition/Large Group/ Small Group II

- Measure the circumference of a large object with a string of yarn (for example, a pumpkin in October). Then as a class find someone or something that is as tall as the object is round.
- During large group time, measure a child with a length of yarn. Have the child look for something or someone in the class that measures the same length as the yarn.
- Trace children's shapes on butcher paper and allow them to measure their shapes and compare to one another. Elicit terms such as taller, shorter, tallest, and shortest.

Tubbing II

- Introduce Cuisenaire Rods to tubbing. Begin to explore how to build steps using only three of the rods at first. Increase the number of rods to determine the tallest and shortest rods.
- Look for students to place them in graduated order.

Center Activities

- science: measurement with the balance scale, selecting familiar objects. Encourage comparisons, for example, which is heavier?

123

- water and sand table: introduce measuring cups, again encouraging comparisons.
- Extend this use of measuring cups to the science center, comparing the weight of one cup of one solid to another, for example, one cup of rice to one cup of flour.
- art: rulers and protractors for creating lines and arcs of various sizes
- blocks: roads and tunnels, ramps
- cooking: cutting/ breaking food items in half and one of the halves in half again, placing the three pieces in graduated order (e.g: pretzels)

EVALUATION/ASSESSMENT

- **concrete:** observations during work with manipulatives, observations of transfer throughout the day, photographs, models
- **pictorial:** matching objects to pattern cards
- **abstract:** drawing or creating a pattern on paper, chalk board, or dry erase board

HANDOUTS/STUDENT WORKSHEETS

Resource A:
Early Childhood Educational Supplies Catalog Resource List
Resource B:
Attendance Chart
Resource C:
"Who is here today?" label
Resource D:
Workmat Grid

RESOURCE A

Early Childhood Educational Materials Catalog Resource List

ABC School Supply, Inc.
1-800-669-4222
Fax: 1-800-933-2987
http://www.abcschoolsupply.com
3312 N. Berkeley Lake Rd.
Box 100019
Duluth, GA 30136-9419

Center for Innovation in Education, Inc. Materials Catalog
1-800-395-6088
Fax: 1-408-741-6290
http://www.best.com/~center
20665 4th Street
Saratoga, CA 95070-5878

Ideal
1-800-845-8149
Fax: 1-800-328-5131
5623 West 115th Street
Alsip, IL 60482-9931

J.L. Hammett Co.
Early Learning Catalog
1-800-333-4600
Fax: 1-800-873-5700
http://www.hammett.com
PO Box 859057
Braintree, MA 02185-9057

Kaplan
1-800-334-2014
Fax: 1-800-452-7526
PO Box 1310
Lewisville-Clemmons Road
Lewisville, NC 27023-0609

Lakeshore Learning Materials
1-800-421-5354
Fax: 1-310-537-5403
2695 E. Dominguez Street
PO Box 6261
Carson, CA 90749

Nasco Fort Atkinson
1-800-558-9595
Fax: 1-414-563-8296
http://www.nascofa.com
901 Janesville Avenue
PO Box 901
Fort Atkinson, WI 53538-0901

orange				
blue				
green				
yellow				
red				
	circle	**heart**	**square**	**triangle**

DIRECTIONS:

1. Make a graph using a 22" x 24" sheet of poster board. For twenty children, draw lines to create five columns and six rows. Each rectangular shape in the matrix should be 3.5" x 5.5".

2. On the far left vertical column, beginning with the top left rectangle, place 3" x 5" construction paper in the rectangular space, one in each of these colors: orange, blue, green, yellow, and red.

3. On the bottom row, leave the far left rectangle blank. Beginning with the second rectangle, trace one of these shapes in each rectangular space: circle, heart, square, triangle.

4. Laminate the graph.

5. Place a one inch square of Velcro [prickly side] on the top of each rectangle in the matrix.

6. Prepare 3" x 5" blank index cards by writing the name of a student on each one. Attach a small replica of the child's symbol on his/her name card as well.

7. Laminate the name/symbol cards.

8. Attach the soft piece of one inch square of Velcro to the top center of each name card.

RESOURCE C
"Who is here today?" Graph

Who is here today?

Resources
and Materials:
Tools for
Implementing
the Core
Knowledge
Preschool
Sequence

Resources and Materials: Tools for Implementing the Core Knowledge Preschool Sequence

TEACHERS: The resources and materials listing that follows is correlated with the general topics, specific competencies and skills included in the Core Knowledge Preschool Sequence. This list is not intended to be either a comprehensive or necessary inventory of materials needed to implement the Core Knowledge Preschool Sequence. Indeed, if yours is an established preschool classroom, you undoubtedly have acquired a wealth of materials over the years. Perhaps, for example, your classroom is well-stocked with role playing materials - masks, costumes, puppets, etc. With a bit of resourcefulness and creativity, you can effectively stimulate and guide children in using these materials to practice many of the oral language competencies included in the Preschool Sequence. You may find it unnecessary to add additional materials to your particular classroom from the Oral Language materials listed below. On the other hand, perhaps you presently have few resources to assist children in developing a sense of time or space and will need to add these particular kinds of materials to your classroom. The listing below of specific games, manipulative materials, children's books, teacher's references, cassettes, and so on is designed to get you started. The names, addresses, telephone and fax numbers of all manufacturers or distributors have been included, whenever possible, for your convenience.

READINESS DIMENSION:
Physical Well-Being and Motor Development
CK PRESCHOOL SEQUENCE TOPIC:
Movement and Coordination

Kids On Stage – charades game encourages children to use pantomime and nonverbal expression *(Childswork/Childsplay: H8426)*

Hopscotch, Hangman, Hot Potato and Hahaha: A Rulebook of Children's Games – by Jack Maguire, Prentice-Hall, 1990

Shadow Play Screen – used to encourage children to move in various ways to develop accurate body image *(Lakeshore: LA289)*

READINESS DIMENSION:
Social and Emotional Development
CK PRESCHOOL SEQUENCE TOPIC:
Autonomy and Social Skills

Children of the World Puzzles – floor puzzles of six different children; multicultural *(Learning Well: NA324447)*

Children's Faces Puzzles – four puzzles of children's faces; multicultural *(Learning Well: NA387041)*

Core Knowledge Social Skills Posters – designed to be used in conjunction with the "Stop and Think" social skills training procedures; posters outline steps for teaching listening, following directions, asking for help, sharing, etc. *(Core Knowledge Foundation)*

How Do You Feel Today? – poster with mirror surrounded with photos of children's faces depicting various emotions *(Lakeshore: LA475)*

Manners – by Aliki; a book to introduce manners *(Michael Olaf: DB10)*

My First Board Games – simple games to introduce turn taking, following game rules *(Learning Well)*

Peacemaking Skills for Little Kids – Class Set – teacher's manual of lessons and activities that address many of the Core Knowledge social skill and conflict resolution goals; also includes a puppet, audio cassette and poster of class rules *(Peace Education Foundation)*

Perfect Pigs – a book to introduce manners, by Brown and Kennedy *(Childswork/Childsplay: H8367)*

Photo Emotion Cards – large photographs of children depicting various emotions *(Learning Well: LL06006)*

Stop and Think Classroom Posters – posters outline the five steps in the "Stop and Think" social skills training *(Roen)*

READINESS DIMENSION:
Approaches to Learning
CK PRESCHOOL SEQUENCE TOPIC:
Work Habits

Classroom Labeling System – peel and stick written labels with color photos to label classroom supplies on shelves, etc.; facilitates classroom organization, children's independence in returning materials to the proper location *(Lakeshore: LA72)*

My Grandmother Went to the Market – game format for building auditory memory needed for following directions, etc.; picture cards aid in remembering and retelling sequence of items grandmother bought at the market (*Child's Play: 6002*)

READINESS DIMENSION:
Language Development
CK PRESCHOOL SEQUENCE TOPIC: Oral Language

RESOURCES FOR PICTURES AND GAMES TO ENCOURAGE ORAL LANGUAGE:

- *Communication Skill Builders*
- *LinguiSystems*
- *SuperDuper*

Descripto Bingo – bingo game designed to encourage children to use adjectives and rich descriptions of pictures (*Super Duper: BK-239*)

Exactly the Opposite, by Tana Hoban; book of photo opposites (*Montessori Services:L650*)

Fun With Opposites Coloring Book (*Dover: 25983-8*)

Getting Dressed Sequence Puzzles – boy or girl; useful for guiding retelling of everyday experiences (*Montessori Services: Y44boy, Y74girl*)

In, On and Under – lotto game for learning prepositional concepts (*Constructive Playthings: CTG-02*)

Little Riddles – picture cards with riddle on the back side of each card; good for developing listening skills (*ABC: 752-01091*)

Opposites – interlocking puzzle cards (*Ravensburger: International Playthings*)

Photo Preposition Cards – photos illustrating in, on, between, etc. (*Montessori 'n Such: LO322*)

Plunk's Pond – clever riddle game for preschoolers; several clues are provided, in decreasing difficulty, for each riddle (*Linguisystems: N20-0P8*)

Reading Readiness Cards – 4 card sets: rhyming, opposites, classifying, sequencing; good buy for large number of cards (*Hammett: 88245D*)

Scenes to Build (Images a Construire) – large, colorful, detailed posters of various scenes; excellent for encouraging children to talk about and describe what they see in the scene; includes guide with teaching suggestions (*Learning Well: 337106*)

Secret Square – game that encourages children to ask questions to determine which picture square is concealing a marker (*Childswork/Childsplay: H8428*)

Social Sequence Sets – set 1 = 3 card photo sequences; set 2 = 4 card photo sequences of every day events (*Montessori 'n Such: LO326, LO 327*)

SPARC for Concepts – flip book of black and white line drawings with specific activities designed to build understanding of basic concepts, such as spatial, temporal and quantitative words (*Linguisystems: 6-0048-1P8*)

Stickers – assorted inexpensive stickers by theme; may be used by child to recreate a verbally described scene (receptive language), to independently create a scene and then describe (expressive language), etc. (*Dover*)

Sticker Scenes – reusable: house, ocean, pirate, jungle, farm, zoo; use as above (*Dover*)

Talking in Sentences – flip book of black and white line drawings to encourage children to construct various kinds of sentences; can also be used for listening activities (*Super Duper: CP-26*)

Tense Sequence Cards – photo cards: past, present, future (*Montessori 'n Such: LO310*)

Uniset Sticker Scenes – airport, fire station, birthday party, house, farm, zoo, sea, story characters (Curious George, Madeline, BusyTown); use as described above

CK PRESCHOOL SEQUENCE TOPIC: Nursery Rhymes, Poems, Fingerplays and Songs

NEARLY ALL OF THE NURSERY RHYMES, POEMS, FINGERPLAYS AND SONGS OF THE PRESCHOOL SEQUENCE ARE INCLUDED IN THE FOLLOWING BOOKS:

- *Big Book for Babies*, by Kay Chorao, *Barnes & Noble, 1998*
- *My First Book of Nursery Rhymes* illustrated by Hilda Offen, *Barnes & Noble, 1993*
- *The Itsy Bitsy Spider*, by Cromwell, Hibner and Faitel, *Partner Press, 1983*
- *Wee Sing Nursery Rhymes and Lullabies*, 1985; *Wee Sing*

THE FOLLOWING BOOKS ARE ALSO GOOD CHOICES:

- *Finger Frolics*, by Cromwell, Hibner and Faitel, *Partner Press, 1983*
- *I'm a Little Teapot and Other Movement Songs*, by Anne Kennedy, *Scholastic, 1994*
- *Mother Goose: A Collection of Classic Nursery Rhymes*, selected and illustrated by Michael Hague, *Henry Holt, 1984*
- *Read Aloud Rhymes for the Very Young*, selected by Jack Pretlusky, *Alfred A. Knopf, 1986*
- *Singing Bee: A Collection of Favorite Children's Songs*, by J. Hart, *Lothrop, Lee and Shephard, 1982*
- *Talking Like the Rain: A First Book of Poems*, by Kennedy and Kennedy, *Brown and Company, 1992*
- *The Merry-Go-Round Poetry Book*, by Nancy Larrick, *Delacorte Press, 1989*
- *The Playtime Treasury*, by P. Corbett, *Doubleday, 1989*

- *The Reader's Digest Children's Songbook*, Reader's Digest Association, 1995
- *The Real Mother Goose*, illustrated by Blanche Fisher Wright, *Checkerboard Press*, 1991
- *Tommie dePaola's Mother Goose*, illustrated by Tommie dePaola, *G.P. Putnam's Sons, 1985*
- *Where is Thumbkin: 500 Activities To Use With Songs You Already Know* by Schiller and Moore, *Gryphon House, 1993 (Kimbo: GH 13156)*; cassette also available
- *Children's Songs and Fingerplays*, 1979, *Price, Stern, Sloan*

CK PRESCHOOL SEQUENCE TOPIC:
Storybook Reading and Storytelling Materials

BIG BOOK RESOURCES FOR THE CORE KNOWLEDGE STORIES, FABLES AND LEGENDS:

The following big books are available from *Rigby*:
- *The Gingerbread Boy*
- *Goldilocks and the Three Bears*
- *The Little Red Hen*

The following big book is available from *Scholastic*:
- *The Town Mouse and the Country Mouse* (also includes *The Lion and the Mouse*)

The following large, illustrated story sequence cards are available from the *Core Knowledge Foundation*:
- *How Turtle Flew South*
- *The Shoemaker and the Elves*
- *Thumbelina*
- *Why Flies Buzz*
- *Betsy Ross and the American Flag*
- *George Washington and the Cherry Tree*
- *Hard Working Abe Lincoln*
- *Martin Luther King, Jr. – A Man of Peace*
- *Thanksgiving*

RESOURCES FOR THE CORE KNOWLEDGE STORYBOOKS:

These books are available from many resources, including most local bookstores. The following resources represent several options.

The following Preschool Sequence titles are available from *Scholastic*:
- *Amazing Grace*
- *Blueberries for Sal*
- *Caps for Sale*
- *The Carrot Seed* (also in Spanish)
- *Corduroy* (also in Spanish)
- *Curious George* (also in Spanish)
- *Goodnight Gorilla*
- *Harold and the Purple Crayon*
- *The Littles*
- *Madeline* (also in Spanish)
- *Make Way for Ducklings* (also in Spanish)
- *The Snowy Day* (also in Spanish)
- *Swimmy*
- *Tikki Tikki Tembo*
- *The Very Hungry Caterpillar*
- *Where the Wild Things Are*

The following Preschool Sequence titles are available from *Amazon.com*:
- *Brown Bear, Brown Bear, What Do You See?*
- *Chicka Chicka Boom Boom*
- *Frederick*
- *Mike Mulligan and His Steam Shovel*
- *Millions of Cats*
- *Miss Rumphius*
- *My Father's Dragon*
- *Runaway Bunny*
- *Sam and the Tigers: A New Retelling of Little Black Sambo*
- *Story of Ferdinand*
- *Strega Nona*
- *Uncle Jed's Barbershop*

The following Preschool Sequence titles are available from *Borders.com*:
- *A Boy, A Dog & A Frog*
- *Are You My Mother?*
- *Ask Mr. Bear*
- *Bobo's Magic Wishes*
- *Cat in the Hat*

- *Good Dog, Carl*
- *Mufaro's Beautiful Daughters*
- *The Park Bench*
- *The Red Balloon*
- *Swimmy*

The following Preschool Sequence titles are available from *Barnes&noble.com*:
- *The Tale of Rabbit and Coyote*

RESOURCES FOR NONFICTION BOOKS:

The following Preschool Sequence titles are available from *Amazon.com*:
- *Children Just Like Me*
- *People*

The following Preschool Sequence titles are available from *Borders.com*:
- *First Discovery*
- *Eye Openers Series*

The following Preschool Sequence titles are available from *Barnes&noble.com*:
- *A Child's Book of Art: Great Pictures, Great Words*

RESOURCES TO EXTEND THE STORYBOOKS:

- *Feltboard backgrounds and characters for Goldilocks and the Three Bears, The Gingerbread Boy, The Little Red Hen and The Three Little Pigs* (Learning Worlds)

- *Flip-Flop Dolls for Goldilocks and the Three Bears, The Three Little Pigs and Thumbelina* (Flip Flop Dolls)

- *Lakeshore and Primary Concepts also carry various kits with storytelling objects.*

CK PRESCHOOL SEQUENCE TOPIC:
Emerging Literacy Skills for Reading and Writing

ABC Cards – several sets of alphabet cards; each letter with different designs for matching (Child's Play: 6001)

Alphabet Activity Posters – large wall posters for each letter; each poster has write and wipe space to include words beginning with that letter that are familiar to the children, such as their first names (Lakeshore: RR432)

Alphabet Matching Game – simple lotto game (*Lakeshore: GT634*)

Alphabet Stamps – manuscript stamps (*Lakeshore: ED1470, ED1471*)

Beaded Alphabet Cards – useful for finger tracing (*ABC School Supplies: 101-45551, 101-50751*)

Build a Book – 90 rubber picture stamps, ink pad and colored pencils to use in completing story starters in an activity book (*Reader's Digest Young Families, Inc.*)

Classroom Labeling System – peel and stick written labels with color photos to label classroom supplies on shelves, etc. (*Lakeshore: LA72*)

Click – high quality magazine for preschoolers that includes related fiction and nonfiction selections (*Cricket*)

Draw and Tell – book of stories to be told aloud by the teacher, as she draws a surprise picture, piece by piece to accompany the story; excellent for encouraging children to retell stories (*Phoenix: 1-55037-032-4*)

Fit-a-Letter – crepe foam rubber letter puzzles for upper or lower case letters; can be used for matching letter to puzzle form or separately: individual, tactile letters; puzzle form (w/out letter) as a "stencil" (*Hammett: 82741D, 92748D*)

I Can (Cut and Stick, Crayon, Draw Animals, Fingerpaint) – by Ray Gibson; four colorful books each with 4-6 step illustrated directions for very simple art and craft activities; (*Amazon.com*)

Ladybug – high quality story magazine for preschoolers, 2-6 (*Cricket*)

Letters and Words, by John Presland and Pam Adams – story and game (*Child's Play: 046-9*)

I Read Signs, I Read Symbols – Tana Hoban books with photographs of signs, symbols; environmental print awareness (*Montessori Services: L655, L652*)

Magnetic Alphabet Letters and Board – upper and lower case (*Discount: MAGUP, MAGLOW, MAGBOD*)

Pretend Soup and Other Real Recipes, by Mollie Katzen; children's cookbook – each recipe accompanied by sequential steps and illustrations; illustrations could be copied and cut apart for sequencing (*Michael Olaf: DR24*)

Reading Readiness Cards – 4 card sets: rhyming, opposites, classifying, sequencing; good buy for large number of cards (*Hammett: 88245D*)

Ready to Read Box – moveable alphabet, objects and word cards; also available in Spanish (*Lakeshore: LC1012*)

Sequence Cards – 30 cards; 2-4 cards/set (*ABC School Supplies: 115-30551*)

Shape-Along – simple step-by-step visual directions for creating pictures with precut, paper shapes; great intro to following "written" directions (*Primary Concepts*)

Write Your Story – coloring book with interesting pictures to stimulate dictation (*Dover: 23732-X*)

PHONEMIC AWARENESS

The following children's books are specifically recommended to help call children's attention to rhyming and the sounds of oral language.

These titles are available from *Scholastic*:
- Barnyard Banter

- **Clap Your Hands**
- **The Cow That Went Oink**
- **I Can't Said the Ant**
- **In a Small, Small Pond**
- **In the Tall, Tall Grass**
- **Jake Baked the Cake**
- **Jamberry**
- **Pigs in the Mud**
- **The Red Hen**
- **Silly Sally**
- **Tumble Bumble**

These titles are available from Amazon.com:
- **Dr. Seuss' ABCs**
- **Down By the Bay**
- **Fox in Socks**
- **Pass the Fritters, Critters**
- **Ride a Purple Pelican**
- **See You Later, Alligator**
- **Sheep in a Jeep**
- **Six Sick Sheep**
- **There's a Wocket in My Pocket**

Articulation Box – small objects representing words that begin with each sound in the alphabet (*Primary Concepts: K1202*)

Myrtle's Beach – riddle game based on detecting initial sounds (*Linguisystems: N22-6P8*)

Ooples and Boonoonoos – by Yopp & Yopp (*Harcourt Brace, ISBN #: 0-15-309028-6*); activity book and cassette using familiar children's songs to build phonemic awareness.

Phonemic Awareness in Young Children, by M. Adams, B. Foorman, I. Lundberg and T. Beeler, Paul H. Brookes, 1998; detailed games for preschool through first grade; also includes assessment tests

Phonemic Awareness – Playing with Sounds to Strengthen Beginning Reading Skills, by V. Fitzpatrick, *Creative Teaching Press, 1997*; quick, simple activities for preschool through second grade

Sound Alikes – miniature objects and playing boards for practicing rhyming words *(Primary Concepts)*

SPARC for Phonological Awareness – flip book of black and white line drawings with specific activities for building phonological awareness skills *(Linguisystems: 6-0164-XP8)*

FINE MOTOR SKILLS, WRITING

(ALSO SEE VISUAL ARTS)

RESOURCES FOR PRACTICING
WRITING STROKES AND LETTERS:

• **Build A Doodle 1 and 2** – books with step-by-step drawings to create simple pictures and designs; good way to incorporate practice of various writing strokes in the Preschool Sequence *(Amazon.com)*

• **Chalkboards** – individual chalkboards *(Lakeshore: KC275)*

• **Drawing With Children**, by Mona Brookes, *G.P. Putnam's Sons, 1996*; describes the "Monart method" developed by the author, with specific activities for children as young as four years old; uses an approach that has similarities to the French ecole maternelle's "graphisme" (teaching of strokes and motifs)

• **Graphisme Atelier** – draw and wipe cards for practicing writing strokes; two levels: premier is good for three year olds, I is appropriate for four year olds. *(Learning Well: 34024, 34016)*

• **Prewriting Motor Skills Boards** – wood stencils for practicing writing letters *(Lakeshore: LA433)*

• **Write and Wipe Dry Erase Boards** – individual size dry erase boards, with markers and erasers *(The Marker Board People)*

RESOURCES FOR CHILD SIZED PRACTICAL LIFE/HOME LIVING MATERIALS FOR FINE MOTOR PRACTICE:

• Michael Olaf
• Montessori 'n Such

Chinese Checkers – with colored small knobbed pegs; good practice for pincer grip, patterns, etc *(Michael Olaf: DT32)*

The Helpful Shoelace, by Pam Adams; storybook with a shoelace and lacing activities for fine motor skills *(Child's Play: 0-85953-297-6)*

Fun With Easy Shapes Stencils – small activity book for tracing *(Dover Publications)*

Lacing Shapes, Lace-A-Puppet – sewing, lacing skills *(Hammett: 82828D, 14920D)*

Sew 'n Sew – wooden sewing toy *(Michael Olaf: DT24)*

READINESS DIMENSION:
Knowledge Acquisition and Cognitive Development
CK PRESCHOOL SEQUENCE TOPIC: Math

KITS:

• **Saxon Pre-K Math Kit** – comprehensive teacher's manual of day-to-day activities that address many of the Preschool Sequence math goals. *(Saxon)*

RESOURCES FOR TEACHERS:

• **More Than Counting** – by Moomaw and Heironymous *(Redleaf Press, 1995)* – practical and engaging activities using teacher made and commercial materials; good ideas for center use or tubbing

SAME-DIFFERENT, MATCHING:

Animal Lotto – simple matching *(Child's Play: 6137)*

Animals Quartet, Little People's Quartet – simple card games for color matching and sorting *(Child's Play: 6006, 6005)*

Art Lotto – matching lotto game with masterpieces from the National Gallery of Art *(Michael Olaf: DA14)*

Domino Circus Matching Game – simple matching *(Discovery Toys: 2510)*

Same and Different Book, by John Presland and Pam Adams – story and game *(Child's Play: 043-4)*

SORTING ,CLASSIFICATION, PATTERNS AND SERIATION:

Attribute Blocks Center – blocks plus book of activities *(Lakeshore: T2304)*

Beads and Pattern Cards – many types, wood or plastic *(ABC School Supplies)*

Colorama – game of different color shapes *(Constructive Playthings: IPI-07)*

Shoe Counters *(T3204)*, **Cat and Dog Counters** *(T5124)*, **Shell Counters** *(T3240)*, **Bug Counters** *(T2324)*, **Frog, Turtle and Lizard Counters** *(T9812)* – miniature plastic objects for sorting and counting *(Lakeshore)*

Count, Sort and Pattern Workmats – provide structure in use of concrete manipulatives *(Lakeshore, T4528)*

Giant Pegboard – no pattern cards; plastic pegs can be stacked and snapped together *(Discovery Toys: 1650)*

Jumbo Classifying Clues – gameboards and picture cards to create double-entry tables *(Hammett: 60523D)*

Miniature Zoo or Farm Animals – 100 animals of 20 varieties; inexpensive ($8) *(Galt: EI460D, EI1434E)*

Patterns by Ivan Bulloch, Thompson Publishing, 1994 - colorful pictures and ideas for finding and making patterns using a variety of materials

Rainbow Links and Pattern Cards – plastic colored links *(ABC School Supplies: 015-51151, 153-15751; Hammett: Ring-o-Links and Pattern Cards (80953D and 80954D)*

Shape, Size and Color Sorting Kit – 360 vinyl shapes in three sizes and five colors, plus vinyl sorting rings that can be used to create manipulative "Venn diagrams"; lots of sorting opportunities for limited expense *(Primary Concepts: SSCS)*

Sequence Size Puzzles – size seriation with crepe foam puzzles, clothing or animal theme *(Hammett: 80852D, 80853D)*

Sequencing Sizes – six image sets of insects which vary progressively in size and can be used for seriation *(Hammett: 64886)*

Sequencer – manipulative shapes of crepe foam rubber, plus pattern sequence cards depicting outline of these shapes: child places shapes directly on cards for initial sequencing practice, etc. *(Hammett: 80509D)*

Stickers – assorted inexpensive stickers; use for making patterns *(Dover)*

Sticker Starters – stickers and workbook set (four books), which focuses on patterns, colors and shapes, counting/numbers, ABC *(Troll: YS989)*

Unifix Cubes Center – cubes plus book of activities *(Lakeshore: T7632)*

SHAPES AND GEOMETRY

(ALSO SEE ORIENTATION IN TIME AND SPACE)

Circles by Frank Nichols – story and game *(Child's Play: 047-7)*

Curves by Frank Nichols – story and game *(Child's Play: 049-3)*

Geoboard Center – six geoboards, rubber bands, book *(Lakeshore: T4516)*

Geometric Shape Stamps – five stamps/set; sets of curved figures and straight figures *(Primary Concepts: GSSC, GSSS)*

Giant Pegboard – no pattern cards; plastic pegs can be stacked and snapped together *(Discovery Toys: 1650)*

Pass the Bag – 3-D shapes and gameboards; children match shapes by touch *(Child's Play: 9695)*

Picture the Pieces – large 3-D puzzle blocks which can be stacked to make six different scenes/puzzles *(Discovery Toys: 2740)*

Puzzle Cards: Match and Mix – three card puzzle to be sequenced (vertically) to make a character *(School Zone)*

Stencils by Frank Nichols – story and game *(Child's Play: 048-4)*

Zoo Cards – puzzle cards to sequence (left to right) to make individual animals in a game format *(Child's Play: 6004)*

MEASUREMENT

Measure Up Cups – plastic stacking cups; good for seriation, measuring, color sorting *(Discovery Toys: 1640)*

Ten Beads Tall by Pam Adams – storybook with square beads to use for measuring height, width and length *(Child's Play: 0-85953-242-9)*

COUNTING

Counters – *Shoe Counters (T3204)*, *Cat and Dog Counters (T5124)*, *Shell Counters (T3240)*, *Bug Counters (T2324)*, *Frog, Turtle and Lizard Counters (T9812)*; miniature plastic objects for sorting and counting *(Lakeshore)*

Count, Sort and Pattern Workmats – provide structure in use of concrete, manipulatives (Lakeshore, T4528)

Albert Moves In – by Annie Kubler; storybook with bead abacus to practice counting *(Child's Play: 0-85953-240-2)*

How Many? – by John Presland and Pam Adams; game and story to practice counting *(Child's Play: 045-0)*

Number Snap – card game for number recognition *(Child's Play: 6000)*

Tactile Numbers – *(Montessori 'n Such-5P)*

Unifix Cubes Center – cubes plus book of activities *(Lakeshore: T7632; Hammett also)*

CK PRESCHOOL SEQUENCE TOPIC: Orientation in Time

Day and Night, Then and Now, Usborne, 1990; two books with many two-page picture layouts to stimulate discussion and comparison *(EDC Publishing)*

Grandma's Day – a story that looks at the past, activities and objects *(Michael Olaf: DH33)*

Long Ago and Today – by Rozanne Williams *(Creative Teaching Press, 1996)* – simple picture book with side by side pictures comparing contemporary life with that long ago

Make Your Own Calendar (*Dover: 24193-9*)

One Hundred Years Ago – by Donna Marriott (*Creative Teaching Press, 1998*) – simple picture book with side by side pictures comparing what things are like today with those one hundred years ago

Sequencing Cards – 3, 4, and 6 image sets showing daily activities; 4 image set showing, step-by-step progression, completion of an object from beginning to end (*Hammett: 58382D, 58383D, 58384D, 70248D*)

Social Sequence Sets – set one has three card photo sequences; set two has four card photo sequences of every day events (*Montessori 'n Such: LO326, LO 327*)

Start to Finish Books (Fruit to Jam, Tree to Table, Cow to Ice Cream) – good for talking about sequential transformations over time (*Amazon.com*)

Teddy Bear Weather – weekly calendar, with focus on the days of the week; includes weather materials; good for three year olds; inexpensive (*ABC: 317-43391*)

Time and Growth Sequence Cards – age, growth, seasons/animals, plant, people (*Montessori 'n Such: NO467*)

Turn of the Century – by Ellen Jackson (*Charlesbridge Publishing, 1998*) – richly illustrated picture book with text explaining daily life from a child's point of view, starting in the year 1000 and progressing in 100 year intervals to the year 2000

Weather Club – peel and stick vinyl weather center; clothing, weather indicators, etc.; traditional activity to use with calendar, especially with reference to "yesterday, today, tomorrow" (*Hammett: 2737ID*)

Year Round Calendar Bulletin Board Set – monthly calendar, with month headings; includes holiday cards; good for four year olds; inexpensive (*ABC: 625-82891*)

CK PRESCHOOL SEQUENCE TOPIC: Orientation in Space

As The Crow Flies: A First Book of Maps, by Gail Hartman, *Aladin Books, 1993* – a clever paperback with very simple maps from the perspective of a rabbit, crow, horse, etc.

Can You Read a Map?, by Rozanne Williams, *Creative Teaching Press, 1996* – inexpensive paperback with 5 very simple maps based on classic fairy tales (The Three Bears, Red Riding Hood, etc.); maps could be used in a number of ways: retell a simple version of the story and ask child to trace the path taken, give oral directions and ask child to point out the path on the map, etc.

Easy Animal Mazes – small activity book; other maze books available – *Easy Mazes, Bird Mazes, Nature Mazes* (*Dover Publications*)

Location Lotto – spatial, directional words and pictures (*ABC School Supplies: 625-53551*)

Lost in Space; Which Way Please? – board games which use elementary grid and map references to help characters find their way home; spatial orientation (*Child's Play: 7567; 7505*)

Little Planner – 3-D shapes and pattern cards; matching; spatial orientation; varying degrees of difficulty (*Leisure Learning Products: 414*)

Me on the Map, by Joan Sweeney; book for 4-6 year olds; young girl's adventure, with focus on maps, starting in her room, neighborhood, town, etc.

Mr. Mighty Mind – 3-D shapes and pattern cards; matching; spatial orientation; varying degrees of difficulty; slightly more difficult than Little Planner (*Leisure Learning Products: 401*)

Parquetry Blocks and Pattern Cards – (*Educational Insights: EI-4601-5P, EI-4600-5P*)

Picture Perfect – clear plastic grid and colored tiles with pattern cards; patterns can be placed directly under grid; different sets of tiles available to make different sequencing patterns (shapes, symbols, numbers, letters) (*Educational Insights: EI-1723-5P*)

Picture Peg – plastic pegboard and pegs, with patterns of increasing difficulty (*Discovery Toys: 2550*)

Puzzle Tiles and Pattern Cards – parquetry (*ABC School Supplies: 247-10251, 752-46051*)

Tan-graphics – crepe foam rubber shapes, plus tangram-like pattern cards; child first matches which shapes are needed to a "match" card and then tries to recombine/arrange the shapes on the outlined "make" card (*Hammett: 556802D*)

Where Is It – spatial relation cards, prepositions (*ABC School Supplies: 103-49951; Hammett: 64884*)

CK PRESCHOOL SEQUENCE TOPIC: Scientific Reasoning and the Physical World

RESOURCES FOR TEACHERS:

• *Bugs to Bunnies*, by Goin, Ripp and Solomon, *Chatterbox Press, 1989* – selective use of activities within one unit, such as the mammal unit that features rabbits; useful in teaching understanding of living world (*Gryphon House*)
• *Everybody Has a Body - Science From Head to Toe*, by Rockwell, Williams and Sherwood,

Gryphon House, 1992 – teacher activity book that is good for exploring all the senses and developing body image *(Gryphon House)*

- **Macmillan Early Science Activities** –used selectively, activities in the following sets cover the topics in the Preschool Sequence: Plants, Garden Science, Color and Light, Air and Water, Five Senses, Our Bodies, Animals; correlated big books with very appealing color photos also available *(Newbridge)*

SCIENCE PICTURE BOOKS FOR CHILDREN:

The titles listed relate in particular to the Preschool Sequence Science goals.

The following titles are available from *Scholastic:*

- **Animal Babies – A Counting Book**
- **Baby Animals**
- **Butterfly**
- **Frog**
- **From Egg to Robin**
- **Water (by S. Canizares)**
- **Water (by F. Asch)**

The following titles are available from *Creative Teaching Press:*

ANIMAL HABITATS
- **At the Farm**
- **At the Pond**
- **At the Seashore**
- **At the Zoo**
- **In a Tree**
- **In the Desert**
- **In the Forest**
- **In the Garden**
- **In the Meadows**
- **In the Park**
- **Underfoot**

ANIMAL CHARACTERISTICS
- **Animal Ears**
- **Animal Eyes**
- **Animal Feathers and Fur**
- **Animal Feet**
- **Animal Mouths**
- **Animal Noses**
- **Animal Skin and Scales**
- **Animal Tails**

PLANT CHARACTERISTICS
- **Plant Blossoms**
- **Plant Fruit and Seeds**

- **Plant Leaves**
- **Plant Stems and Roots**
(Also see Newbridge Publishing for nonfiction big books and picture books))

OTHER RESOURCES:

Montessori 'n Such Catalogue – carries an excellent variety of photo cards, puzzles, books and manipulatives on science related topics

Animal Coloring Books – inexpensive books of birds, ocean animals, farm animals, etc. *(Dover)*

Animals of the World – six sets of small animal models (6/set) for different habitats *(Michael Olaf: DP47/*forest, *DP48/* jungle, *DP49/*ocean, *DP98/*farm)

Animal Rummy Card Games – decks of ocean animals, endangered species, etc. *(Montessori Services)*

Animal Stickers – inexpensive thematic sets: ocean, birds, fish, wild animals, etc. *(Educational Insights)*

Human Cycle – book on how humans are born, grow, age, meet needs *(Michael Olaf: DP74)*

Miniature Zoo or Farm Animals – 100 animals of 20 varieties; inexpensive ($8) *(Galt: EI460D, EI1434E)*

CK PRESCHOOL SEQUENCE TOPIC: Music

Shrink-wrapped sets of these CDs may be purchased directly from the Core Knowledge Foundation.

CK Preschool Sequence instrumental music included on:

- **Baby Dance:** Bizet, Overture from Carmen; Khachaturian, Sabre Dance; Strauss, Thunder and Lightning Waltz
- **Classics for Kids:** Brahams, Cradle Song (Lullaby); Herbert,

March of the Toys; Tchaikovsky, selections from Nutcracker; Villa-Lobos, Little Train

- **Naxos 8.550885:** Schumann, Kinderszenen; Tchaikovsky, Album for the Young; Debussy, Children's Corner Suite, Schumann, Dreams; Debussy, Golliwog's Cakewalk
- **Naxos 8.550924:** Can-Can and Other Dances from the Opera – Offenbach, Can-Can; Ponchielli, Dance of the Hours
- **Naxos 8.550258**: Mozart Sonatas, etc. - Variations on "Ah, vous dirai-je maman!"

RESOURCES FOR TEACHERS:

- **Music and Movement in the Classroom**, by Steven Traugh, *Creative Teaching Press, 1993*; thirty written lessons, with two cassettes of accompanying music by Steve and Greg; lessons include activities focusing on rhythm, moving to music of different tempo and intensity, using gestures to accompany fingerplays and songs, etc.
- **The I Can't Sing Book for Grownups Who Can't Carry a Tune, But Want to Do Music with Young Children** – by Jackie Silberg *(Gryphon House, 1998)* – simple activities that address many of the Preschool Sequence music goals

(For CK Preschool Sequence songs, see Nursery Rhymes, Poems, Fingerplays and Songs)

Get set...Go!, by Sally Hewitt, *Children's Press, 1994*; four simple paperback books with ideas and simple instructions for creating sound effects, as well as string, percussion and wind instruments

Hear the World Sound Lotto – cassette of music, animals, sounds matched to photo scenes *(Discovery Toys: 2370)*

Listening Lotto-ry – several sets: environmental sounds, animal sounds, musical instruments *(Educational Insights)*

135

Preschool Playtime Band – perky marching music including Yankee Doodle, Stars and Stripes, Alexander's Ragtime Band, etc.; cassette *(KIM 9099C)*

Rhythm Band for Little People – children accompany music on cassette with their rhythm instruments by following coded instrument chart *(Kimbo: KIM 0840C)*

Rhythm Instruments – inexpensive instruments ($2-$8); selection includes rhythm sticks, triangle, castanets, finger cymbals, sand blocks, maracas, bells, etc. *(Montessori 'n Such)*

Simple Folk Dances – easy to learn dances appropriate for preschoolers; cassette *(Kimbo: KIM 07042C)*

Simplified Rhythm Stick Activities – cassette of popular songs for "tapping the beat" *(KIM 2015C)*; rhythm sticks also available *(ACC 2015 – Kimbo)*

Sound Stories – "stories" told by sequences of sounds; children simultaneously sequence corresponding pictures *(Montessori n' Such: LO339)*

Sound Track Around the World – tape of sounds (elephant from India, drummers from Africa, etc.) and lotto game *(Michael Olaf: DT02)*

Spotlight on Violin, Spotlight on Piano – tapes highlighting classical selections with these instruments; set also includes flute and guitar *(Michael Olaf: DM11)*

Walk Like the Animals – music to encourage rhythmic movements like different animals; cassette *(Kimbo: KIM 7040C)*

CK PRESCHOOL SEQUENCE TOPIC: Visual Arts

CK Preschool Sequence art prints are available as a set from:

• **Art Print Resources**

(Also, The Metropolitan Museum of Art carries a glazed earthenware reproduction or soft sculpture of "Blue Hippo," *FO322K*)

RESOURCES FOR TEACHERS:

Discovering Great Artists: Hands-On Art for Children in the Styles of the Great Masters, by MaryAnn Kohl and Kim Solga, *Bright Ring Publishing, 1996*; includes sculpting, painting and drawing activities for children ages 4-12. Exact titles of works of art do not necessarily correspond to the works of the Preschool Sequence. However, this may still be a helpful resource for stimulating ideas for teachers who have little experience in calling children's attention to elements of art and attempting to recreate them in their own works *(Gryphon House)*.

Drawing With Children, by Mona Brookes, *G.P. Putnam's Sons, 1996* – describes the "Monart method" developed by the author, with specific activities for children as young as four years old; uses an approach that has similarities to the French ecole maternelle's "graphisme" (teaching of strokes and motifs)

Let Out the Sunshine – A Montessori Approach to Creative Activities, by Regina Barnett, *Wm. C. Brown Publishers, 1981* – simple step-by-step art activities for practice in tearing, cutting, gluing, modeling, etc. *(Michael Olaf)*

Scribble Cookies and Other Independent Creative Art Experiences for Children, by Mary Ann Kohl, *Bright Ring Publishing, 1985* – simple activities using a variety of techniques and media

OTHER RESOURCES:

A Child's Book of Art: Great Pictures, First Words, by Lucy Micklethwait *(New York: Dorling Kindersley, 1993)*; large color prints organized by subject, content; no commentary, just words as labels "family," "pets," etc. – perfect for preschoolers; other titles by Lucy Micklethwait in the *I Spy* or *Spot A* series are equally appropriate for preschoolers

Degas' Little Dancer, by Laurence Anholt, *Barron's, 1996*; beautifully illustrated picture book will enhance young children's appreciation of the story behind Degas' sculpture of the "Little Fourteen Year Old Dancer"

I Can (Cut and Stick, Crayon, Draw Animals, Fingerpaint) – by Ray Gibson – 4 colorful books, each with 4-6 step directions for making simple arts and craft projects *(Amazon.com)*

Marie in Fourth Position – by A. Littlesugar *(Penguin Putnam Books, 1996)* – engaging story with lovely illustrations that explains the story behind Degas' sculpture of the "Little Fourteen Year Old Dancer"; paperback

National Gallery Art Lotto – matching and memory game with art masterpieces *(Montessori 'n Such: AO759)*

Amazon.com
1-800-201-7575

Barnes&noble.com
1-800-843-2665

Borders.com
1-800-770-7811

ABC School Supply, Inc.
1-800-669-4222
Fax: 1-800-933-2987
  3312 N. Berkeley Lake Rd.
  Box 100019
  Duluth, GA 30136-941

Art Print Resources
1-800-466-6799
Fax: 1-914-964-6799
  209 Riverdale Avenue
  Yonkers, NY 10705

Child's Play
1-800-639-6404
Fax: 1-800-854-6989
  67 Minot Avenue
  Auburn, ME 04210

Childswork/Childsplay
1-800-962-1141
Fax: 1-610-277-4556
  100 Plaza Drive
  Seacaucus, NJ 07094

Communication Skillbuilders
1-800-211-8378
Fax: 1-800-232-1223
  555 Academic Court
  Berkeley, CA 94709

Constructive Playthings
1-800-832-0572
  1227 East 119th Street
  Grandview, MO 64030

Core Knowledge Foundation
1-800-238-3233
Fax: 1-804-977-0021
  801 East High Street
  Charlottesville, VA 22902

Creative Teaching Press
1-800-444-4287
  P.O. Box 6017
  Cypress, CA 90630

Cricket Magazine Group
1-800-827-0227
  P. O. Box 300
  Peru, IL 61354

Discount School Supply
1-800-627-2829
Fax: 1-800-879-3753
  P. O. Box 7636
  Spreckels, CA 93962

Discovery Toys
1-800-426-4777
  Martinez, CA 94553
  (call for the nearest distributor)

Dover Publications
1-516-294-7000
  31 East 2nd Street
  Mineola, NY 11501

Educational Insights
1-800-995-4436
  16941 Keegan Ave.
  Carson, CA 90746

Flip Flop Dolls
1-540-662-3932
Fax: 1-540-662-9083
  401 South Stewart Street
  Winchester, VA 22601

Galt
1-800-966-4258
Fax: 1-203-265-4730
  63 N.Plains Industrial Rd.
  Wallingford, CT 06492

Gryphon House
1-800-638-0928
Fax: 1-301-595-0051
  P. O. Box 207
  Beltsville, MD 20704

J.L. Hammett
1-800-333-4600
Fax: 1-800-873-5700
  P. O. Box 9057
  Braintree, MA 02184

Kimbo
1-800-631-2187
Fax: 1-908-870-3340
  P. O. Box 477
  Long Branch, NJ 07740

PUBLISHERS' NAMES
AND ADDRESSES *CONTINUED*

Lakeshore Learning Materials
1-800-421-5354
  P. O. Box 6261
  Carson, CA 90749

Learning Well
1-800-645-6564
Fax: 1-800-413-7442
  111 Kane Street
  Baltimore, MD 21224

Learning Wonders
1-888-407-7182
  501 Talbott Drive
  Wilmore, KY 40390

LinguiSystems
1-800-776-4332
  3100 4th Avenue
  East Moline, IL 61244

Marker Board People
1-800-828-3375
Fax: 1-888-882-3298
  1611 North Grand River
  Lansing, MI 48906

Metropolitan Museum of Art
1-800-468-7386
  255 Gracie Station
  New York, NY 10028

Michael Olaf
1-707-826-1557
Fax: 1-707-826-2243
  P. O. Box 1162
  Arcata, CA 95518

Montessori 'n Such
1-800-287-1985
Fax: 1-703-760-9720
  2821F Dorr Avenue
  Fairfax, VA 22031

Montessori Services
1-707-579-3003
Fax: 1-707-579-1604
  836 Cleveland Avenue
  Santa Rosa, CA 95401

Music Matters
1-800-216-6864
  409 Blandwood Avenue
  Greensboro, NC 27401

Peace Education Foundation
1-800-749-8838
Fax: 1-305-576-3106
  1900 Biscayne Boulevard
  Miami, FL 33132

Phoenix Publications
1-800-221-1274

Primary Concepts
1-800-660-8646
Fax: 1-510-486-1248
  Box 10043
  Berkley, CA 94709

Newbridge Educational Publishing
1-800-867-0307
Fax: 1-609-786-4417
  P. O. Box 6002
  Delran, NJ 08370

Rigby
1-800-822-8661
Fax: 1-800-427-4429
  P. O. Box 797
  Crystal Lake, IL 60039

Roen Educational Distributors
1-941-293-8894
Fax: 1-941-297-3358
  P. O. Box 2156
  Winter Haven, FL 33883

Saxon Publishers
1-800-284-7019
  2450 John Saxon Boulevard
  Norman, OK 73071

Scholastic
1-800-724-6527
Fax: 1-573-635-5881
  2931 East McCarty Street
  Jefferson City, MO 65101

Super Duper Publications
1-800-277-8737
Fax: 1-800-978-7379
  P. O. Box 24997
  Greenville, SC 29616

Troll
1-800-247-6106
  101 Corporate Drive
  Mahwah, NJ 07430

bibliography

Bibliography

Achieving the Goals – Goal 1: All Children in American Will Start School Ready to Learn. Washington, DC: U.S. Department of Education, 1995.

Adams, G. and Englemann, S. *Direct Instruction Research.* Seattle, WA: Evergreen Press.

Adams, G. and Sandfort, J. *First Steps, Promising Futures: State Kindergarten Initiatives in the Early 1990s.* Washington, DC: Children's Defense Fund, 1994.

Alexander, R., Rose, J. and Woodhead, C. *Curriculum Organisation and Classroom Practice in Primary Schools – A Discussion Paper.* London: Department of Education and Science, 1992.

All Children Ready to Learn. Washington, DC: U.S. Department of Education, 1993.

Approaching Kindergarten: A Look at the Preschoolers in the United States. Washington, DC: U.S. Department of Education, 1995.

Arnold, D. and Whitehurst, G. *Accelerating Language Development Through Picture Book Reading: A Summary of Dialogic Reading and its Effects* in Dickinson, D., ed. *Bridges to Literacy.* Cambridge, MA: Blackwell Publishers, 1994.

As the Twig is Bent . . . Lasting Effects of Preschool Programs (The Consortium for Longitudinal Studies). Hillsdale, NJ: L. Erlbaum Publishers, 1983.

Baker, A. and Piotrkowski, C. *The Effects of Participation in HIPPY on Children's Classroom Adaptation: Teacher Ratings – An Initial Report of the NCJW Center for the Child.* New York: National Council of Jewish Women, 1993.

Baron, L. *Du Mouvement au Trace en Petite Section.* Paris: Magnard, 1993.

Baron, L. *Du Trace au Graphisme en Moyenne Section.* Paris: Magnard, 1994.

Baudis, A. and Clapies, D. *Grapho-motricite Avec les 2/3 Ans.* Paris: Nathan, 1992.

Beals, D., DeTemple, J. and Dickinson, D. *Talking and Listening that Support Early Literacy Development of Children From Low Income Families* in Dickinson, D., ed. *Bridges to Literacy.* Cambridge, MA: Blackwell Publishers, 1994.

Beals, D. and Tabors, P. *Arboretum, Bureaucratic and Carbohydrates: Preschoolers Exposure to Rare Vocabulary at Home. First Language*, 15, (1995), 57-76.

Beck, I. and Juel, C. *The Role of Decoding in Learning to Read. American Educator.* 19, (1995), 8, 21-25.

Berenger, L. *Pour Une Pedagogie Reussie de la Langue.* Paris: Nathan, 1987.

Berk, L. and Winsler, A. *Scaffolding Children's Learning: Vygotsky and Early Childhood Education.* Washington, DC: NAEYC, 1995.

Bertouy, E. *La Petite Section d'Ecole Maternelle: Une Pedagogie par Objectifs.* Paris: L'Ecole, 1985.

Bertouy, E. *La Grande Section d'Ecole Maternelle: Une Pedagogie par Objectifs.* Paris: L'Ecole, 1992.

Bertouy, E. et Cordonni, R. *La Moyenne Section d'Ecole Maternelle: Une Pedagogie par Objectifs.* Paris: L'Ecole, 1989.

Blank, M., Rose, S. and Berlin, L. *The Language of Learning: The Preschool Years.* New York: Grune and Stratton, 1978.

Bouvry, S. *Livret d'Observation et d'Evaluation – Cycle 1.* Paris: Nathan, 1993.

Boyer, E. *Ready to Learn: A Mandate for the Nation.* Princeton, NJ: Carnegie Foundation for the Advancement of Teaching, 1991.

Bredekamp, S. ed. *Developmentally Appropriate Practice in Early Childhood Programs Serving Children From Birth Through Age 8.* Washington, DC: NAEYC, 1987.

Bredekamp, S. *Reflections on Reggio Emilia. Young Children*, 49, (1993), 13-17.

Bredekamp, S. and Rosegrant, T. ed. *Reaching Potentials: Appropriate Curriculum and Assessment for Young Children.* Washington, DC: NAEYC, 1992.

Bredekamp, S. and Rosegrant, T. ed. *Reaching Potentials: Transforming Early Childhood Curriculum and Assessment.* Washington, DC: NAEYC, 1995.

Cahen, J. *Langage Avec les 3/4 Ans.* Paris: Nathan, 1990.

Campbell, F. and Ramey, C. *Cognitive and School Outcomes for High-Risk African-American Students at Middle Adolescence: Positive Effects of Early Intervention, American Educational Research Journal*, 32, (1995), 743-772.

Caring Communities: Supporting Young Children and Families. Alexandria, VA: National Association of State Boards of Education, 1992.

Celeste, Bernadette. *Les Petits a la Maternelle.* Paris: Syros-Alternatives, 1992.

Champdavoine, L. *Ecoute et Regarde.* Paris: Nathan, 1983.

Cochran-Smith, M. *The Making of a Reader.* Norwood, NJ: Ablex Publishing, 1984.

Cycle des Apprentissages Premiers: Aide a l'Evaluation

des Eleves. Volumes 1 and 2. Minstere de l'Education Nationale, Direction des Ecoles. Douai: Imprimerie Nationale.

Cycle des Apprentissages Premiers: Cycle 1: Livret Scolaire. Volumes 1 and 2. Minstere de l'Education Nationale, Direction des Ecoles. Douai: Imprimerie Nationale.

Daufresne, M., Hoffman, Y. and Jehan, E. *Decouverte de l'Ecrit Avec les 2/3 Ans.* Paris: Nathan, 1994.

Dickinson, D., ed. *Bridges to Literacy.* Cambridge, MA: Blackwell Publishers, 1994.

Dickinson, D.K. and Smith, M.W. *Longterm Effects of Preschool Teachers' Book Reading on Low Income Children's Vocabulary and Story Comprehension. Reading Research Quarterly,* 29, (1994), 105-122.

Dicktelmiller, M., Jablon, J., Dorfman, A. Marsden, D. and Meisels, S. *The Work Sampling System Teacher's Manual.* Ann Arbor, MI: Rebus Planning Associates, 1994.

Dodge, D. and Colker, L. J. *The Creative Curriculum for Early Childhood.* Washington, DC: Teaching Strategies, Inc., 1992.

Duthoit, M. *L'enfant et l'ecole: Aspects synthetiques du suivi d'un echantillon de vingt mille eleves des ecoles. Education et Formations,* 1988, no. 16. 3-13 (Ministere de l'Education Nationale).

Early Childhood Programs: Promoting the Development of Young Children in Denmark, France and Italy. Washington, DC: General Accounting Office, 1995.

L'Ecole Avant Six Ans. Paris: Bordas (Collection R. Tavernier), 1984.

L'Ecole Maternelle. Paris: Ministere de l'Education Nationale, 1986.

L'Ecole Maternelle et Sa Pedagogie. Meeting Proceedings, Montreal-San Francisco, May 2-13, 1994. Organized by Michel Forget, Inspector, Ministere de l'Education Nationale. Presenters: Theresa Boisdon, President of AGIEM, Jeane-Pierre Niant, Teacher-Trainer, Avallon.

Education in France. Ministere de l'Education Nationale, Vanves: DEP October, 1993.

Edwards, C., Gandini, L. and Forman, G. *The Hundred Languages of Children: The Reggio Emilia Approach to Early Childhood Education.* Norwood, NJ: Ablex Publishing Corporation, 1993.

Epstein, A., Schweinhart, L. and McAdoo, L. *Models of Early Childhood Education.* Ypsilanti, MI: High/Scope Press, 1996.

L'Etat de l'Ecole, No. 2, MEN-DEP, (October 1992).

Ferrand, M.ed. *Approches de la Langue Orale a l'Ecole Maternelle.* 1994. Lyons, France: CRDP

French, L. *Preschool Images from Korea* in *Education Week,* June 7, 1995, 33, 35.

French, L. and Song, M. J. *Images from Korean Kindergartens: Supporting the Acquisition of Preacademic Skills through Developmentally Appropriate Teacher-Directed Approaches.* Unpublished Paper.

Friedrich, Jean-Marie, Helwig, Christinae, Jenger, Yvette. *Livret de l'Enseignant – Cycle 1.* Paris: Nathan, 1993.

Galinsky, E., Howes, C., Kontos, S. and Shinn, M. *The Study of Children in Family Child Care and Relative Care: Highlights of Findings.* New York: Families and Work Institute, 1994.

Gallagher, J. and Ramey, C., eds. *The Malleability of Children.* Baltimore, MD: Paul H. Brookes Publishing Co., 1987.

Gallistel, C.R. *The Organization of Learning.* Cambridge, MA: MIT Press, 1990.

Gallistel, C.R. and Gelman, R. *Preverbal and Verbal Counting and Computation. Cognition,* 44, (1992), 43-77.

Gandini, L. *Fundamentals of the Reggio Emilia Approach to Early Childhood Education. Young Children,* 49, (1993), 4-8.

Geary, D. *Teacher's Guide: Mathematics.* Unpublished paper prepared for the Core Knowledge Foundation, 1996.

La Geographie de l'Ecole. Ministere de l'Education Nationale. Vanves: DEP, February, 1993.

Getman, D. *Basic Montessori: Learning Activities for Under Fives.* Bromley, England: Christopher Helm Publishers, 1987.

Got, V. *Langage Avec les 4/5 Ans.* Paris: Nathan, 1993.

Grunwald, L. *The Amazing Minds of Infants. Life,* 16 (July, 1993), 46-50.

Guidelines for Appropriate Curriculum Content and Assessment in Programs Serving children Ages 3 Through 8. Position Statement of NAEYC and NAECS/SDE. Washington, DC: NAEYC, 1990.

Guillard, G., Hibon, M., Lelievre-Bourdin, L., Monier, R., Tavernier, R. and Venon, F. *Les Chemins de l'Ecriture.* Paris: Bordas, 1988.

Hart, B. and Risley, T. *Meaningful Differences in the Everyday Experiences of Young American Children.* Baltimore: Paul H. Brookes, 1995.

Healy, J. *Endangered Minds: Why Children Don't Think and What We Can Do About It.* New York: Simon and Schuster, 1990.

Homann, M., Banet, B and Weikart, D. *Young Children in Action: A Manual for Preschool Educators.* Ypsilanati, MI: High/Scope Press, 1979.

Hoffman, M. and Weikart, D. *Educating Young Children.* Ypsilanati, MI: High/Scope

Press, 1995.

Jablon, J., Marsden, D., Meisels, S., and Dichtelmiller, M. *The Work Sampling System Omnibus Guidelines: Preschool – Third Grade.* Ann Arbor, MMI: Rebus Planning Associates, 1994.

Jager-Adams, M. *Beginning to Read: Thinking and Learning About Print – A Summary.* Champaign, IL: University of Illinois, Center for the Study of Reading, 1990.

Jager-Adams, M. and Bruck, M. *Resolving the Great Debate. American Educator.* 19, (1995), 7, 10-21.

Jarousse, Jean Pierre, Mingat, Alain et Richard, Marc. *La Scolarisation Maternelle a Deux Ans: Effets Pedagogiques et Sociaux* in *Education and Formations,* 31 (April/June, 1992), 2-9.

Jenger, Y. *Comptines Rythmees, Comptines Crees Avec les 3/4 Ans.* Paris: Nathan, 1995.

Jett-Simpson, M. *Parents and Beginning Reading.* Atlanta: Humanics Ltd, 1984.

Jolibert, J. et Crepon, C., ed. *Former des Enfants Lecteurs,* volumes 1 and 2. Paris: Hachette, 1984.

Kagan, S. *Readiness 2000: Rethinking Rhetoric and Responsibility. Phi Delta Kappan,* December, 1990, 272-279.

Kagan, S. *Readiness Past, Present and Future: Shaping the Agenda. Young Children,* 48 (1992), 48-52.

Karweit, N. *The Effects of a Story Reading Program on the Vocabulary and Story Comprehension Skills of Disadvantaged Prekindergarten and Kindergarten Children.* Washington, DC: U.S. Dept. of Education (Center for Research on Elementary and Middle Schools), 1989.

Karweit, N. *The Effect of Story Reading on the Language Development of Disadvantaged Prekindergarten and Kindergarten Students* in Dickinson, D., ed. *Bridges to Literacy.* Cambridge, MA: Blackwell Publishers, 1994.

Labenne, J. *En Maternelle – Guide a l'Usage des Debutants.* Paris: Armand Colin, 1993.

Laying the Foundation for School Success: Recommendations for Improving Early Learning Programs. Baltimore: Maryland Department of Education, 1992.

Leclerq, S. *Scolarisation Precoce: Un Enjeu.* Paris: Nathan, 1995.

Lentin, L. *Appredre a Parler – tome 1.* Paris: Les Editions ESF, 1987.

Lentin, L. *Ces Enfants Qui Veulent Apprendre.* Paris: Quart Monde, 1995.

Lentin, L. *Comment Apprendre a Parler a l'Enfant (tome 2).* Paris: Les Editions ESF, 1973.

Les Cycles a l'Ecole Primaire. Ministere de l'Education Nationale de la Jeunesse et des Sports Direction Des Ecoles. Paris: Hachette, 1991.

Les'Ecoles du Premier Degre: 1994-1995. Ministere de l'Education Nationale. Vanves: DEP, January, 1995.

Les Eleves de Nationalite Etrangere Scolarises Dans Le Premier et Le Second Degre en 1993-1994. Ministere de l'Education Nationale. Vanves: DEP, January, 1995.

Les Petits: La Section des 2 a 4 Ans. Paris: Bordas (Collection R. Tavernier), 1989.

Levenstin, P. *Messages from Home: The Mother-Child Home Program and the Prevention of School Disadvantage.* Columbus, OH: Ohio State University Press, 1988.

Levenstin, P. *The Mother-Child Home Program: Research Methodology and the Real World* in McCord, J. and Tremlay, R., eds. *Preventing Antisocial Behavior: Interventions from Birth Through Adolescence.* New York: Guilford Press, 1992.

Levenstin, P. and O'Hara, J. *The Necessary Lightness of Mother-Child Play* in MacDonald, K., ed. *Parents-Child Play: Descriptions and Implications.* Albany, NY: SUNY Press, 1993.

Livrets Scolaires/Feuilles d'Evaluation de: Lycee Francais International Laperouse, San Francisco, CA; L'Academie de Grenoble, Grenoble, France; L'Academie de Strasbourg, Strasbourge, France.

Lombard, A. *Success Begins at Home.* Lexington, MA: Lexington Books. 1981.

Love, J. M., Logue, M. E., Trudeau, J. V. and Thayer, K. *Transitions to Kindergarten in American Schools – Final Report of the National Transition Study.* Portsmouth, NH: RMC Research Corporation, 1992.

Lovejoy, M. and Westheimer, M. *Voices from the Field: A Case of One Inner City HIPPY Program.* New York: National Council of Jewish Women, 1993.

Lundberg, I., Frost, J. and Peterson, O. P. *Effects of an Extensive Program for Stimulating Phonological Awareness in Preschool Children. Reading Research Quarterly,* 23, (1988), 264-284.

Madden, J., Levenstein, P., Levenstein, S. *Longitudinal IQ Outcomes of the Mother-Child Program, Child Development,* 47 (1976), 1015-1025.

Maclean, M., Bryant, P., and Bradley, L. *Rhymes, Nursery Rhymes and Reading in Early Childhood. Merrill-Palmer Quarterly,* 33, (1987) 255-281.

Malaguzzi, L. *For An Education Based on Relationships. Young Children,* 49 (1993), 9-12.

Malegue, C. *La Vie a l'Ecole des Enfants de Niveau Preelementaire* in *Education and Formations* 11 (April/June, 1987), 11-24.

Mandler, J. *A New Persepective on Cognitive Development in Infancy.* **American Scientist,** 78 (May/June, 1990), 236-243.

Maryland's Primary Assessment System. Baltimore: Maryland Department of Education, 1995.

Mason, J., Peterman, C. and Kerr, B. *Reading to Kindergarten Children* in Strickland, D. and Morrow, L., eds. ***Emerging Literacy: Young Children Learn to Read and Write.*** Newark, DE: International Reading Association, 1989.

McGill-Frazen, A. *What Does "Developmentally Appropriate" Mean?* **Effective School Practices,** 12 (1993), 55-57.

McMahan, I. *Public Preschool From the Age of Two: The Ecole Maternelle in France.* **Young Children,** 47 (5), 1992, 22-28.

Meisels, S. *Uses and Abuses of Developmental Screening and School Readiness Testing.* **Young Children,** 42 (1987), 4-8; 68-73

Morrow, L. **Literacy Development in the Early Years: Helping Children Read and Write.** Englewood Cliffs, NJ: Prentice-Hall, 1989.

Morrow, L. *Retelling Stories: A Strategy for Improving Children's Comprehension, Concept of Story Structure and Oral Language Complexity.* **The Elementary School Journal,** 85 (1985), 647-661.

Meyer, G., Larois, D. L'Heritier, E., Mackowiak, M. **Cheminement en Maternelle.** Paris: Hachette, 1991.

National Education Goals Report: Building a Nation of Learners. Washington, DC: National Education Goals Panel, 1995.

NAEYC Position Statement on Developmentally Appropriate Practice in the Primary Grades, Serving Five through Eight Year Olds in **Young Children,** 43 (1988), 140-144.

NAEYC Position Statement on School Readiness in **Young Children,** 46 (1990), 21-23.

Ninio, A. and Bruner, J. *The Achievement and Antecedents of Labeling.* **Journal of Child Language,** 5 (1978), 5-15.

Olmstead, P. and Weikart, D. ***Families Speak: Early Childhood Care and Education in 11 Countries.*** Ypsilanti, MI: High/Scope Press, 1994.

Olmstead, P. and Weikart, D. **How Nations Serve Young Children.** Ypsilanti, MI: High/Scope Press, 1989.

Peak, L. **Learning to Go to School in Japan: The Transition From Home to Preschool Life.** Berkeley: University of California Press, 1991.

Pierre, R., Terrieux, J. and Babin, N. ***Orientations–Projets–Activites Pour l'Ecole Maternelle.*** Paris: Hackette, 1992.

Plaisance, E. *Les sciences sociales et la petite enfance.* **Revue de l'Institut de Sociologie.** 1994, no. 1-2, 69-84.

Programmes de l'Ecole Primaire. March 10, 1995. Ministere de l'Education Nationale, Paris.

Ramey, C. and Campbell, F. *The Carolina Abecedarian Project: An Educational Experiment Concerning Human Malleability* in Gallagher, J., and Ramey, C. **The Malleability of Children.** Baltimore, MD: Paul H. Brookes Company, 1987.

Ramey, C., McGinness, G., Collier, A., Barrie-Blackley, S. *The Abecedarian Approach to Social Competence: Cognitive and Linguistic Intervention for Disadvantaged Preschoolers* in Borman, K., ed., **The Social Life of Children in a Changing Society.** Hillsdale, NJ: L. Erlbaum Associates, 1982, 145-174.

Ramon, S. **Schema Corporel Avec les 3/4 Ans.** Paris: Nathan, 1992.

Reconsidering Children's Early Development and Learning: Toward Common Views and Vocabulary. Washington, DC: National Education Goals Panel, 1995.

Regenstein, M., Silow-Carroll, S. and Meyer, J. **Early Childhood Education: Models for Expanding Access.** Washington, DC: Economic and Social Research Institute, 1995.

Review of Research on Achieving the Nation's Readiness Goal - Technical Report. Washington, DC: U.S. Department of Education, 1993.

Richardson, G. and Marx, E. **A Welcome For Every Child: How France Achieves Quality in Child Care: Practical Ideas for the United States.** New York: The French American Foundation, 1989.

Richmond Montessori School Curriculum Guide. Unpublished paper, Richmond, VA: Richmond Montessori School.

Schickendanz, J., Chay, S., Gopin, P., Sheng, L., Somg, S., and Wild, N. *Preschoolers and Academics: Some Thoughts.* **Young Children,** 36 (1990), 4-13.

Schumaker, J. and Sherman, J. *Parent as Intervention Agent* in Schiefelbush, R., ed. **Language Intervention Strategies.** Baltimore: University Park Press, 1978.

Schweinhart, L. *Lasting Benefits of Preschool Programs.* **ERIC DIGEST,** January, 1994. Urbana, IL: ERIC Clearinghouse on Elementary and Early Childhood Education.

Schweinhart, L., Barnes, H. and Weikart, D. **Significant Benefits: The High/Scope Perry Preschool Study Through Age 27.** Ypsilanti, MI: High/Scope Press, 1993.

Schweinhart, L., Weikart, D. and Larner, M. *Consequences of three preschool curriculum models through age 15.* **Early Childhood Research Quarterly,** 1 (1986), 15-45.

Seefeldt, C., ed. **The Early Childhood Curriculum, A Review of Current Research.** New York: Teacher's College

Press, 1992.

Sentihes, I. *Parle-Moi!* Paris: Quart Monde, 1988.

Sharpe, R. *To Boost IQs, Aid Is Needed in First Three Years. Wall Street Journal,* April 12, 1994.

Slavin, R., Kareweit, N. and Wasik, R. *Preventing Early School Failure: Research, Policy and Practice.* Boston: Allyn and Bacon, 1994.

Slaughter, J. *Beyond Storybooks: Young Children and the Shared Book Experience.* Newark, DE: International Reading Association,1993.

Snow, C. *Conversations With Children* in Fletcher, P. and Garman, M,, eds. *Language Acquisition.* New York: Cambridge University Press, 1986.

Snow, C., Burns, S. and Griffin, P., eds. *Preventing Reading Difficulties in Young Children.* Washington, DC: National Academy Press, 1998.

Snow, C. and Ninio, A. *The Contracts of Literacy: What Children Learn From Learning to Read Books* in Teale, W. and Sulzby, E., eds., *Emergent Literacy: Writing and Reading.* Norwood, NJ: Ablex Publishing, 1986.

Spodek, B. *Early Childhood Curriculum and Cultural Definitions of Knowledge* in Spodek, B. and Saracho, O., *Issues in Early Childhood Curriculum.* New York: Teacher's College Press, 1991.

Starting Points in Maryland: Building Collaboration to Promote School Readiness in Young Children. Baltimore: Ready at Five, 1996.

Starting Points – Meeting the Needs of Our Youngest Children. New York: Carnegie Corporation of New York, 1994.

Stewig, J. *Teaching Language Arts in Early Childhood.* New York: CBS College Publishing, 1982.

Strickland, D. and Taylor, D.

Family Storybook Reading: Implications for Children, Families and Curriculum in Strickland, D. and Morrow, L., eds. *Emerging Literacy: Young Children Learn to Read and Write.* Newark, DE: International Reading Association, 1989.

Teale, W. *Home Background and Young Children's Literacy Development* in Teale, W. and Sulzby, E., eds., *Emergent Literacy: Writing and Reading.* Norwood, NJ: Ablex Publishing, 1986.

Teale, W. *Reading to Young Children: Its Significance for Literacy Development* in Goelman, H., Oberg, A. and Smith, F., eds. *Awakening to Literacy.* Exeter, NH: Heineman Educational Books, 1984, 110-121.

Tobin, J., Wu, D. and Davidson, D. *Preschool in Three Cultures: Japan, China and the United States.* New Haven: Yale University Press, 1989.

van der Eyken, W. *The Education of Three-to-Eight Year Olds in Europe in the Eighties.* Great Britain: NFER-Nelson Publishing Company, 1982.

Vezzoli-Clapies, D. and Baudis, A. *Graphomotricite Avec les 3/4 Ans.* Paris: Nathan, 1994.

Viadero, D. *Table Talk* in *Education Week,* December 14, 1994, 35-37.

Villani, J. *Fiches d'Activites Graphiques.* Paris: Nathan, 1985.

Washington, V., Johnson, V., and McCraken, J. *Grassroots Success – Preparing Schools and Families for Each Other.* Washington, DC: NAEYC, 1995.

Watson, R. *Rethinking Readiness for Learning* in Olson, D., ed., *Handbook of Education and Human Development: New Models of Learning, Teaching and Schooling.* London: Blackwell, 1996.

Weikart, D. P. and Schweinhart, L. *The High/Scope Curriculum for Early Childhood Care and Education* in Roopnarine, J. and Johnson, J. eds., *Approaches to Early Childhood Education.* New York: Merrill, 1993, 195-208.

Weisberg, P. *Direct Instruction in the Preschool. Education and Treatment of Children.* 11 (1988), 349-363.

Whitebook, M., Phillips, D., and Howes, C. *Who Cares? Child Care Teachers and the Quality of Care in America: National Child Care Staffing Study.* Oakland, CA: Child Care Employee Project, 1989.

Woodhead, M. *Preschool Education in Western Europe: Issues, Policies and Trends.* New York: Longman, 1979.

Years of Promise: A Comprehensive Learning Strategy for America's Children. New York: Carnegie Corporation of New York, 1996.

appendices

Appendix A:
Reviewers of
Initial Drafts
of the Core
Knowledge
Preschool
Sequence

Appendix A: Reviewers of Initial Drafts of the Core Knowledge Preschool Sequence

The initial draft of the Core Knowledge Preschool Sequence was reviewed by, among others, the following distinguished experts:

Dr. Marilyn Jager Adams

Visiting Scholar
Graduate School of Education
Harvard University

Adjunct Professor
Department of Cognitive and
**   Linguistic Sciences**
Brown University

Adjunct Professor
Center for Reading Research
Stavanger College, Norway

DR. ADAMS received her Ph.D. in cognitive and developmental psychology from Brown University and has been working on issues of education and cognition ever since. In 1995, she was presented with the American Education Research Association's Sylvia Scribner Award for Outstanding Contribution to Education Through Research. In addition to publishing numerous journal articles and book chapters, she is also the author of Beginning to Read: Thinking and Learning about Print. This book, commissioned by the U.S. Department of Education, provides a comprehensive examination and critique of beginning reading practices in light of theory and research in education, psychology, and linguistics. Adams is also the principal author of the primary levels of a new classroom reading program, Collections for Young Scholars (Open Court), and of Odyssey: A Curriculum for Thinking, an experimentally validated program on thinking skills, originally developed for Venezuelan barrio students. She has also developed a diagnostic test of decoding

skills and has co-authored a book on how preschool and kindergarten teachers can help children develop phonemic awareness.

Adams is currently the Vice-President of the American Education Research Association. Other professional affiliations and appointments include serving on the National Academy of Science's Study Committee for the Prevention of Reading Difficulties, the College Board's Advisory Committee for Research and Development, the Consortium on Reading Excellence, the Neuhaus Education Center, The Orton Dyslexia Society, and the Society for Scientific Studies in Reading. She is the literacy consultant for Sesame Street. She also is or has been a member of the Editorial Advisory Boards for a variety of journals, including Applied Psycholinguistics, Language Arts, Journal of Educational Psychology, Memory and Cognition, Reading Research Quarterly, Scientific Studies of Reading and The Reading Teacher.

Dr. Lucia French

Associate Professor of Education
**   and Human Development**
University of Rochester

DR. FRENCH, who received her Ph.D. from the University of Illinois at Champaign-Urbana, is a developmental psychologist with interests in the cognitive and language development of young children. She has co-authored two books and has published and lectured extensively on these facets of early childhood development. She received a Fulbright-Hays Research Fellowship to study early childhood education in Korea in 1991-1994. Observations in Korea sensitized

Dr. French to the important role that receptive language skills and attention management skills play in academic achievement. Since returning from Korea, Dr. French has helped to establish a Head Start Demonstration Center where teachers implement both a process-curriculum, focusing on attention management, listening comprehension, problem solving and communication, and a content-curriculum that presents hands-on science activities enabling children to learn about the world around them using scientific reasoning.

Dr. French has served on the Editorial Board of Child Development. She is also a member of the Society for Research in Child Development, American Educational Research Association, Jean Piaget Society, American Psychological Society and the National Association for the Education of Young Children.

Dr. David C. Geary

Professor of Psychology
University of Missouri
**   at Columbia**

DR. GEARY received his Ph.D. in developmental psychology from the University of California at Riverside. He has held faculty positions at the University of Texas at El Paso and the University of Missouri at Rolla in addition to his current position. He has published more than 60 scientific articles on a variety of topics and has authored one book, Children's Mathematical Development. His research currently focuses on the source and nature of the mathematical achievement gap comparing East Asian nations, specifically China and the United States; cognitive and neuropsychological deficits that contribute to arithmetic-related learning disabilities; changes in cognitive performance in adult aging; and, the application of the principles of evolutionary biology to understanding human social and cognitive development.

Dr. Craig Ramey

**Professor of Psychology
Pediatrics, Sociology and
Maternal and Child Health
University of Alabama
at Birmingham
Director of Civitan
International Research
Center**

DR. RAMEY is a developmental psychologist with a 25 year speciality in early intervention to prevent or treat disabilities in children. He received his Ph.D. in lifespan developmental psychology from West Virginia University and completed postdoctoral research on human learning mechanisms at the University of California at Berkeley. He joined the faculty at the University of Alabama in 1990 after 20 years on the faculty of the University of North Carolina at Chapel Hill.

He has developed systems-based theoretical models of early development that emphasize the dynamic interactions of risk and protective factors in intellectual development especially during the first 8 years of life. These models have been tested in numerous long term intervention studies. He is the founding Director of the Abecedarian Project and Project CARE - two programs that have demonstrated the efficacy of prevention of developmental disabilities in high-risk samples. For example, the Abecedarian Project has reported prevention of intellectual declines and associated academic competence in reading and mathematics through age 15 attributable to preschool intervention. More recently, Dr. Ramey was the founding director of the Infant

Health and Development Program, a successful 8-site randomized controlled trial of early intervention. Presently, he is directing research and evaluation of a 31-site, randomized trial of education reform for 12,000 children in a study known as the Head Start/Public School Transition Demonstration Project.

He has published extensively in the area of early intervention, written over 175 scientific and educational articles and edited two books on high risk children and children with disabilities.

Dr. Sandra Scarr

**Former Chief Executive Officer
KinderCare Learning Centers,
Inc.
Commonwealth Professor of
Psychology
University of Virginia**

DR. SCARR, who received her Ph.D. in Psychology and Social Relations at Harvard University, has held faculty positions as Professor of Psychology at Yale University and the University of Minnesota; she was also the Kerstin Hesselgren Visiting Professor in Sweden. Her research on behavior genetics, intelligence, and child development has been published in more than 200 articles and four books on intelligence, child care, and family issues. In 1985, she won the National Book Award of the American Psychological Association for Mother Care/Other Care. She has received two awards for her research contributions: The Distinguished Contributions to Research and Public Policy Award (American Psychological Association, 1989) and the James McKeen Cattell Award (American Psychological Society, 1993).

She has been elected a Fellow of the American Academy of Arts and Sciences, the American Association for the Advancement of Science, the American Psychological Society and the American Psychological

Association. She has served as editor or on the Editorial Board of several professional journals, including Current Directions in Psychological Science, Developmental Psychology and American Psychologist. She also has served on the Steering Committee on Prevention Research for the National Institute of Mental Health, and has been a consultant to many organizations to improve early education, child care, and family relations.

147

Appendix B:
Ten Years
Later –
Developmentally
Appropriate
Practice: What
Have We
Learned?

Appendix B: Ten Years Later – Developmentally Appropriate Practice: What Have We Learned?

Ten years after the National Association for the Education of Young Children [NAEYC] published its profoundly influential position statement on what it termed *developmentally appropriate practice* [DAP] for preschool and early elementary settings, new influences in the field of early childhood education have recently prompted it to issue a different statement from its 1987 predecessor.

The NAEYC's 1987 document became one of the most widely disseminated educational publications ever, with over half a million copies of the position statement and several million summary brochures distributed throughout the United States. The guidelines enormously influenced beliefs and practices in curriculum design and instruction in early childhood settings. Over the years, the term also acquired strong emotional overtones, becoming a virtual litmus test of one's educational philosophy.

Meanwhile, however, research in cognitive development and how children learn has changed our understanding of child development. Studies of early childhood practices in other countries, which differ significantly from those in the U. S., have revealed significant shortcomings in the approach advocated in 1987.

The 1987 document reflected the exploding number of young children in day care and preschool settings in the United States, as more and more women entered the work force. The lack of state or federal regulations for these settings often meant no training of caregivers and a wide variety of experiences offered to young children.

To establish quality and consistency in preschool programs, NAEYC developed criteria by which preschools and day care settings might seek distinction through a national accreditation process. The 1987 position statement was issued to elaborate on the accreditation guidelines and facilitate their implementation. In particular, it was designed to address the tendency of inexperienced caregivers to simply push down academic curricula originally intended for children in the elementary grades.

The principles that became known as the 1987 DAP had their roots in certain philosophical and educational traditions, ranging from Jean Jacques Rousseau's romanticism to Piagetian constructivism and maturationist psychology. These traditions gave rise to a view of child development as a process that evolved naturally. Young children were said to construct understanding and knowledge through their own independent exploration of the physical world, passing through certain universal developmental stages that occurred at fairly set ages and in a predictable sequence. Formal instruction and outside intervention by adults were regarded as unnecessary and disruptive. Development and readiness to learn could not be hastened or artificially induced; instead, let nature take its course and allow children "to bloom when they were ready." It was necessary to wait for certain skills and competencies to develop before the child was deemed ready to learn.

Since each child independently constructed his own knowledge, appropriate educational practice focused on the individual child. Curriculum emphasized process and discovery. The content learned was considered secondary, even incidental, to how the child learned. Emphasis was placed on developing each child's self-expression and creativity. To foster discovery and freedom of expression, teachers were encouraged to act as if there are no right or wrong answers. Activities were to be child-initiated; the teacher's role was that of facilitator, preparing and providing an appropriate environment. It was deemed especially important that experiences and materials be concrete, manipulative and relevant.

The NAEYC juxtaposed examples of appropriate and inappropriate practice as part of the 1987 position statement. Unfortunately, these led to a polarized, "either/or" view of educational practice and seemed to suggest that there was only one right way to work with young children. For example, appropriate practice was described as allowing "children [to] select many of their own activities," while inappropriate practice was defined as "the teacher direct[ing] activities, deciding what children will do and when." Many teachers concluded that under no circumstances was the teacher to plan or lead activities. As a result, in many preschool settings across the United States, activities became not just child-initiated, but child-dominated. When taken to extremes, each individual child was encouraged to pursue only his own inclinations in the name of independently constructing knowledge. In most instances, there were no clear goals and children were not held to any expectations, boundaries or limits. Furthermore, little attention was paid to helping children function in a classroom setting, learning to sometimes defer the immediate gratification of one's own needs for the benefit of the group.

Another example characterized DAP experiences as active, concrete and manipulative. In practice, this was often interpreted to mean that all abstract or symbolic activities were inappropriate. In many instances, "paper and pencil" activities, as well as any other abstract academic experiences, were systematically withheld from young children.

The overall effect of the 1987 DAP guidelines at the preschool level has been to create a widening gap between preschool and elementary school experiences for most children. Rather than provide an introduction to the world of school, developmentally appropriate preschools often have taught a set of expectations and behaviors that subsequently do not apply in kindergarten. It's little wonder that in recent years kindergarten teachers throughout the U.S. consistently describe entering students as less and less ready for academic instruction than in the past.

Meanwhile, new knowledge about child development has come from research, as well as international comparisons. Animal research and human case studies have significantly advanced our understanding of the cognitive development of the young child, particularly the role of experience upon brain development. It is now clear that each child's physical brain structure reflects his everyday experiences. The presence or lack of experiences in a very real sense shapes the actual physical structure of the brain. The essential connections between brain cells, dendrites, are either elaborated through branching, if stimulated through certain experiences, or eliminated through pruning, if not stimulated. Ultimately, physical brain structure, determined by early experience, affects how the brain will function and learn.*

Other research has led to a more complete understanding of how and when children learn certain knowledge and skills. Researchers using laboratory-controlled conditions have demonstrated that the ages originally established by Piaget as marking the various developmental stages consistently underestimate young children's capabilities. Furthermore, it is also now evident that while some learning, such as early language and awareness of simple quantities, does develop naturally in an automatic, universal fashion for all children, as Piaget suggested, other unnatural learning, such as more sophisticated language, reading and so on, does not develop naturally. Indeed, it very much depends on experience.**

As research demonstrates the limitations of a strict Piagetian view of child development, there is growing interest in the child development theories of the Russian psychologist Lev Vygotsky, who emphasized the role of language development and social interaction in cognitive development. Unlike Piaget, who focused upon the child's independent construction of knowledge, Vygotsky's sociocultural view acknowledges the importance of a child's interaction with others, adults or older peers, who mediate and support the child's learning experiences.†

In addition to research findings, exposure to preschool practices in other countries has called into question many of the assumptions and principles advocated in the name of DAP. American researchers and educators visiting other countries consistently see preschool children doing things that Americans have claimed preschool children are not capable of performing. There are common features in the preschool practices of many developed nations, among them France, Japan and Korea, where students consistently outperform American students academi-

cally in later grades.

In these countries, young children are seen as highly competent and they are held to certain expectations. Furthermore, certain experiences are seen as so critical in the development of all children that they are explicitly specified in written national standards for preschool education. In sharp contrast to the approach promulgated by DAP, preschool practices in these countries are based on the belief that learning requires effort. There is little talk of learning as natural or easy. Instead of focusing solely upon the individual child, attention is paid to helping each child develop personal independence and responsibility within a social context. Finally, while much activity and learning is concrete, manipulative and active, a conscious effort is made to help children make the transition to more symbolic, abstract approaches.

One last lesson from international experience is particularly noteworthy. For many years, Great Britain resisted the practice of most other European countries of explicitly specifying educational expectations and standards. In 1967, the British Department of Education issued the Plowden Report in which it formally adopted progressive education as its approach in early childhood settings. The report described progressive education as child-directed and teacher-facilitated, with an emphasis on learning through discovery and play. Also recommended was an integrated approach through the project method and a rejection of drill and rote learning. In 1992, however, the same Department of Education issued a new report. Alarmed by academic performance that fell consistently below that of students in other developed nations — one international comparison of science achievement indicated that 61 percent of British schools scored below the lowest scoring

Japanese schools – education officials resoundingly rejected progressive education, citing its implementation as the downfall of British academic performance. A national curriculum with explicit standards was established instead.

The British experience with progressive education seems to parallel our own recent history with DAP. Concern is growing here over the ongoing decline in American academic performance at all grade levels. Of particular interest in the search for solutions is Project Follow Through, the massive – over 75,000 children in 170 communities – federally-funded evaluation of various educational approaches used to teach disadvantaged children in grades K-3. This research assessed the children's academic achievement, as well as cognitive and affective development, in light of the instructional approach used. Of all the approaches evaluated, the basic skills model, with a focus on specific instruction in explicitly identified academic and social skills – the model of instruction attacked by supporters of DAP over the years as being developmentally inappropriate – consistently surpassed the other models in terms of student performance in basic skills and in measures of cognitive and affective development. Those models that met DAP criteria were consistently inferior to the basic skills model.††

Given the developments of the last ten years, it is no surprise that NAEYC has reconsidered what constitutes developmentally appropriate practice. Its revised position statement includes the following changes:

• Curriculum addresses both process and content: "Clearly, people in the decades ahead will need fully developed literacy and numeracy skills, and these abilities are key goals of the educational process. In science, social studies (which includes history and geography), music and the visual arts, physical education and health, children need to acquire a body of knowledge and skills. . . . Besides knowledge and skills, *children must develop positive dispositions and attitudes. They need to understand that effort is necessary for achievement*" (italics added).

• The teacher is no longer just a facilitator, but an active participant, using a continuum of teaching strategies ranging from child-initiated to teacher-directed, and planning experiences so that children attain key goals.

• The need to extend manipulative experiences to the level of symbolic representation is recognized: "DAP programs provide opportunities for children to broaden and deepen their behavioral knowledge by providing a variety of firsthand experiences and *helping children acquire symbolic knowledge through representing their experiences in a variety of media, such as drawing, painting, construction of models, [and] dramatic play ...*" (italics added).

Perhaps most important is the conscious effort to eliminate the polarizing "either/or" categorization of practices. Teachers are prompted to recognize that children need both choices and clear definitions of limits, both structure and spontaneity, experiences that challenge and those that practice previously acquired skills.

On paper at least, the NAEYC 's more moderate theoretical position is more consistent with the concepts embodied by Core Knowledge. The challenge now rests with early childhood teachers to translate the principles into practice.

BY LINDA BEVILACQUA,
*Director, Early Childhood Program
Core Knowledge Foundation*

NOTES

*For a lay person's description of brain development, see: Nash, M., "Fertile Minds – A Special Report," Time, vol. 149, no. 5 (February, 1997), pp.48-56; and Healy, J. Endangered Minds: Why Children Don't Think and What We Can Do About It. 1990. New York: Simon & Schuster.

**For a summary of research that calls into question Piagetian theory, see Mandler, J. "A New Perspective on Cognitive Development in Infancy." American Scientist, 78 (May/June, 1990), pp. 236-243.

† For a thorough discussion of Vygotskian theory and its differences from Piagetian theory, see Berk, L. & Winsler, A. Scaffolding Children's Learning: Vygotsky and Early Childhood Education. 1995. Washington, DC: NAEYC.

†† For a discussion of Project Follow Through, see the entire issue of Effective School Practices, vol. 15, no.1 (Winter, 1996).

Reprinted from Common Knowledge, Volume 10, No. 1/2, Winter/Spring'97.

Grade K

Overview
of Topics

Language Arts

I. Reading and Writing
    A. Book and Print Awareness
    B. Phonemic Awareness
    C. Decoding and Encoding
    D. Reading and Language Comprehension
    E. Writing and Spelling
II. Poetry
    A. Mother Goose and Other Traditional Poems
    B. Other Poems, Old and New
III. Fiction
    A. Stories
    B. Aesop's Fables
    C. American Legends and Tall Tales
    D. Literary Terms
IV. Sayings and Phrases

History and Geography

World:
I. Geography: Spatial Sense
II. An Overview of the Seven Continents

American:
I. Geography
II. Native American Peoples, Past and Present
III. Early Exploration and Settlement
    A. The Voyage of Columbus in 1492
    B. The Pilgrims
    C. July 4, "Independence Day"
IV. Presidents, Past and Present
V. Symbols and Figures

Visual Arts

I. Elements of Art
    A. Color
    B. Line
II. Sculpture
III. Looking at and Talking about Works of Art

Music

I. Elements of Music
II. Listening and Understanding
III. Songs

Mathematics

I. Patterns and Classification
II. Numbers and Number Sense
III. Money
IV. Computation
V. Measurement
VI. Geometry

Science

I. Plants and Plant Growth
II. Animals and Their Needs
III. The Human Body
IV. Introduction to Magnetism
V. Seasons and Weather
VI. Taking Care of the Earth
VII. Science Biographies

Appendix C: Kindergarten Goals

Language Arts: Kindergarten

I. Reading and Writing

A. BOOK AND PRINT AWARENESS

- Know parts of a story (for example, title, beginning, end) and their functions.
- Know that print goes from left to right across the page and from top to bottom down the page, and that words are separated by spaces.
- Follow print, pointing to each word from left to right, when listening to familiar stories or other texts read aloud.

B. PHONEMIC AWARENESS

TEACHERS: Phonemic awareness is the understanding that the sound of a word consists of a sequence of smaller, individual sounds. These basic speech sounds that make up words are called phonemes. For example, there are three phonemes in the word "mat": /m/ /a/ /t/. Phonemes are written within back slashes: for example, when you see /b/, you should say neither "bee" nor "buh," but instead a short, clipped "bh" sound. To *segment* is to take words apart into separate syllables or phonemes. To *blend* is to put together separate syllables or phonemes.

NOTE: The technical term "rime" is not the same as "rhyme" in poetry.

- Given a spoken word, produce another word that rhymes with the given word.
- Orally segment words into syllables and demonstrate understanding of syllable breaks by such means as, for example, clapping hands on each syllable or placing a different colored marker to represent each syllable.
  Example: "muffin" ➔ "muf" *[clap]* + "fin" *[clap]*
- Orally blend syllables into words.
  Example: "muf" + "fin" ➔ "muffin"
- Orally blend onsets (any initial consonant or consonant cluster) and rimes (the vowel and any following consonants) in spoken words.
  Example: /c/ - / at/ ➔ cat
  /s/ - /it/ ➔ sit
- Orally blend isolated sounds into a spoken one-syllable word.
  Example: /c/ - /u/ - /p/ ➔ cup
- Given prompting with a picture, isolate and repeat the initial or final sound of a one-syllable spoken word.
  Example: bat ➔ /b/   bird ➔ /d/

NOTE: Some programs insist upon using only the letter sounds and not the letter names. This may be a useful practice in the early stages of learning, in order to avoid confusion between the names of the letters and the speech sounds they represent. For instance, h ("aitch") does not sound like /h/, and w ("double-u") does not sound like /w/. But outside the classroom, most adults will use the letter names, and most children "learn their ABCs"—that is, the letter names—very early. The important goal is to make sure the child understands through consistent performance the difference between speech sounds and their letter names.

C. DECODING AND ENCODING

TEACHERS: Decoding is the act of turning the letters into the speech sounds they represent. Encoding is the act of turning the sounds of spoken language into the corresponding written letters. Children need to understand that the sequence of sounds in a spoken word is represented by a left-to-right sequence of letters in a written or printed word. Through regular and systematic practice, decoding and encoding should become automatic, thus allowing the child to focus attention instead on meaning.

In abbreviations such as CVC, C stands for "consonant" and V stands for "vowel." A CVC word is a consonant-vowel-consonant word, such as "cat" or "mop." An example of a CCVC word is "frog." An example of a CVCC word is "tent."

- Recognize and name all uppercase and lowercase letters of the alphabet. [See Note]
- Match a letter to a spoken phoneme.
  Example: *Teacher says* /b/. *Child points to letter card with* b.
- Decode a letter into the phoneme it represents.
  Example: *Teacher shows letter card* b. *Child says* /b/.

- Write the correct letters to represent a sound or sequence of sounds, up to three consonants or two consonants and a short vowel sound.

  Example: *Spoken by teacher:* /s/   *Written by child:* s

      Spoken by teacher: /m/ /b/ /m/   *Written by child:* m b m

      Spoken by teacher: /b/ /i/ /b/   *Written by child:* b i b

- Read any three-sound CVC word (for example, cat, sit) or nonsense word (for example, mup, fap).
- Read simple phrases or sentences made up of the phonemes mastered so far.

  Example: "Cat ran up." "Sam sat."
- Begin to read VCC, CVCC, and CCVC words with adjacent consonants and short vowel sounds (for example, ant, milk, frog).
- Begin to recognize common words by sight, including *a, the, I, my, you, is, are.*

D. READING AND LANGUAGE COMPREHENSION

- Understand and follow oral directions.
- Tell in his or her own words what happened in stories or parts of stories, and predict what will happen next in stories.
- Distinguish fantasy from realistic text.
- Listen to and understand a variety of texts, both fiction and nonfiction.

E. WRITING AND SPELLING

- Write his or her own name (first and last).
- Write all uppercase and lowercase letters of the alphabet.
- Use letter-sound knowledge to write simple words and messages, consistently representing initial and final consonant sounds (for example, writing "boat" as "bot").

NOTE: Children should read aloud with someone outside of school at least 10 minutes daily.

II. Poetry

TEACHERS: Children should be introduced to a varied selection of poetry with strong rhyme and rhythm. Children should hear these rhymes read aloud, and should say some of them aloud. Some rhymes may also be sung to familiar melodies. The poems listed here represent some of the most popular and widely anthologized titles; children may certainly be introduced to more Mother Goose rhymes beyond the selection below. Whereas children are not expected to memorize the following rhymes, they will delight in knowing their favorites by heart, and will experience a sense of achievement and satisfaction in being able to recite some of the rhymes.

NOTE REGARDING PRESCHOOL CONTENT: Some of the poems and stories specified here are appropriate for preschoolers. Indeed, one would hope that most preschoolers would come to kindergarten having heard, for example, some Mother Goose rhymes or the story of "Goldilocks and the Three Bears." However, as not all children attend preschool, and as home preparation varies, the Core Knowledge Sequence offers a core of familiar rhymes and stories for all kindergarten children. See also the Core Knowledge Preschool Sequence, available from the Core Knowledge Foundation.

A. MOTHER GOOSE AND OTHER TRADITIONAL POEMS

A Diller, A Dollar	Mary, Mary, Quite Contrary
Baa, Baa, Black Sheep	Old King Cole
Diddle, Diddle, Dumpling	Old Mother Hubbard
Early to Bed	One, Two, Buckle My Shoe
Georgie Porgie	Pat-a-Cake
Hey Diddle Diddle	Rain, Rain, Go Away
Hickory, Dickory, Dock	Ride a Cock-Horse
Hot Cross Buns	Ring Around the Rosey
Humpty Dumpty	Rock-a-bye, Baby
It's Raining, It's Pouring	Roses Are Red
Jack and Jill	See-Saw, Margery Daw
Jack Be Nimble	Simple Simon
Jack Sprat	Sing a Song of Sixpence
Ladybug, Ladybug	Star Light, Star Bright
Little Bo Peep	There Was a Little Girl
Little Boy Blue	There Was an Old Woman Who Lived in a Shoe
Little Jack Horner	This Little Pig Went to Market
Little Miss Muffet	Three Blind Mice
London Bridge Is Falling Down	

B . OTHER POEMS, OLD AND NEW

April Rain Song (Langston Hughes)
Happy Thought (Robert Louis Stevenson)
I Do Not Mind You, Winter Wind (Jack Prelutsky)
Mary Had a Little Lamb (Sara Josepha Hale)
The More It Snows (A. A. Milne)
My Nose (Dorothy Aldis)
Rain (Robert Louis Stevenson)
Three Little Kittens (Eliza Lee Follen)
Time to Rise (Robert Louis Stevenson)
Tommy (Gwendolyn Brooks)
Twinkle Twinkle Little Star (Jane Taylor)

III. Fiction

TEACHERS: While the following works make up a strong core of literature, the content of the language arts includes not only stories, fables, and poems, but also the well-practiced, operational knowledge of how written symbols represent sounds, and how those sounds and symbols convey meaning. Thus, the stories specified below are meant to complement, not to replace, materials designed to help children practice decoding skills (see above, I. Reading and Writing).

The following works constitute a core of stories for this grade. In kindergarten, these stories are meant to be read-aloud selections. Expose children to many more stories, including classic picture books and read-aloud books. (In schools, teachers across grade levels should communicate their choices in order to avoid undue repetition.) Children should also be exposed to non-fiction prose: biographies, books on science and history, books on art and music, etc. And, children should be given opportunities to tell and write their own stories.

A. STORIES

The Bremen Town Musicians (Brothers Grimm)
Chicken Little (also known as "Henny-Penny")
Cinderella (Charles Perrault)
Goldilocks and the Three Bears
How Many Spots Does a Leopard Have? (African folk tale)
King Midas and the Golden Touch
The Legend of Jumping Mouse (Native American: Northern Plains legend)
The Little Red Hen
Little Red Riding Hood
Momotaro: Peach Boy (Japanese folk tale)
Snow White and the Seven Dwarfs
The Three Billy Goats Gruff
The Three Little Pigs
A Tug of War (African folk tale)
The Ugly Duckling (Hans Christian Andersen)
The Velveteen Rabbit (Margery Williams)
selections from *Winnie-the-Pooh* (A. A. Milne)
The Wolf and the Kids (Brothers Grimm)

B. AESOP'S FABLES

The Lion and the Mouse
The Grasshopper and the Ants
The Dog and His Shadow
The Hare and the Tortoise

NOTE: Children will read more American legends and tall tales in grade 2.

C. AMERICAN FOLK HEROES AND TALL TALES
Johnny Appleseed
Casey Jones

D. LITERARY TERMS

TEACHERS: As children become familiar with stories, discuss the following:

author
illustrator

IV. Sayings and Phrases

TEACHERS: Every culture has phrases and proverbs that make no sense when carried over literally into another culture. For many children, this section may not be needed; they will have picked up these sayings by hearing them at home and among friends. But the sayings have been one of the categories most appreciated by teachers who work with children from home cultures that differ from the standard culture of literate American English.

A dog is man's best friend.
April showers bring May flowers.
Better safe than sorry.
Do unto others as you would have them do unto you.
The early bird gets the worm.
Great oaks from little acorns grow.
Look before you leap.
A place for everything and everything in its place.
Practice makes perfect.
[It's] raining cats and dogs.
Where there's a will there's a way.

History and Geography: Kindergarten

TEACHERS: In kindergarten, children often study aspects of the world around them: the family, the school, the community, etc. The following guidelines are meant to broaden and complement that focus. The goal of studying selected topics in World History in Kindergarten is to foster curiosity and the beginnings of understanding about the larger world outside the child's locality, and about varied civilizations and ways of life. This can be done through a variety of means: story, drama, art, music, discussion, and more.

The study of geography embraces many topics throughout the Core Knowledge Sequence, including topics in history and science. Geographic knowledge includes a spatial sense of the world, an awareness of the physical processes that shape life, a sense of the interactions between humans and their environment, an understanding of the relations between place and culture, and an awareness of the characteristics of specific regions and cultures.

WORLD HISTORY AND GEOGRAPHY

I. Geography: Spatial Sense (working with maps, globes, and other geographic tools)

TEACHERS: Foster children's geographical awareness through regular work with maps and globes. Have students regularly locate themselves on maps and globes in relation to places they are studying. Children should make and use a simple map of a locality (such as classroom, home, school grounds, "treasure hunt").

- Maps and globes: what they represent, how we use them
- Rivers, lakes, and mountains: what they are and how they are represented on maps and globes
- Locate the Atlantic and Pacific Oceans.
- Locate the North and South Poles.

II. An Overview of the Seven Continents

TEACHERS: Help children gain a beginning geographic vocabulary and a basic sense of how we organize and talk about the world by giving names to some of the biggest pieces of land. Introduce children to the seven continents through a variety of media (tracing, coloring, relief maps, etc.), and associate the continents with familiar wildlife, landmarks, etc. (for example, penguins in Antarctica; the Eiffel Tower in Europe). Throughout the school year, reinforce names and locations of continents when potential connections arise in other disciplines (for example, connect Grimm's fairy tales to Europe; voyage of Pilgrims to Europe and North America; story of "Momotaro—Peach Boy" to Asia [Japan]; study of Native Americans to North America).

NOTE: In later grades, children will continue to learn about all the continents as well as specific countries and peoples.

- Identify and locate the seven continents on a map and globe:
  Asia
  Europe
  Africa
  North America
  South America
  Antarctica
  Australia

AMERICAN HISTORY AND GEOGRAPHY

<u>TEACHERS:</u> The study of American history begins in grades K-2 with a brief overview of major events and figures, from the earliest days to recent times. A more in-depth, chronological study of American history begins again in grade 3 and continues onward. The term "American" here generally, but not always, refers to the lands that became the United States. Other topics regarding North, Central, and South America may be found in the World History and Geography sections of this Sequence.

I. Geography

- Name and locate the town, city, or community, as well as the state where you live.
- Locate North America, the continental United States, Alaska, and Hawaii.

II. Native American Peoples, Past and Present

<u>TEACHERS:</u> As children progress through the grades of the Core Knowledge Sequence, they will learn about many different Native American peoples in many different regions. In kindergarten, study at least one specific group of Native Americans: explore how they lived, what they wore and ate, the homes they lived in, their beliefs and stories, etc., and also explore the current status of the tribe or nation. You might explore a local or regional tribe or nation, and compare it with one far away.

- Become familiar with the people and ways of life of at least one Native American tribe or nation, such as:
  Pacific Northwest: Kwakiutl, Chinook
  Plateau: Nez Perce
  Great Basin: Shoshone, Ute
  Southwest: Dine [Navajo], Hopi, Apache
  Plains: Blackfoot, Comanche, Crow, Kiowa, Dakota, Cheyenne, Arapaho, Lakota (Sioux)
  Northeast: Huron, Iroquois
  Eastern Woodlands: Cherokee, Seminole, Delaware, Susquehanna, Mohican, Massachusett, Wampanoag, Powhatan

III. Early Exploration and Settlement

A. THE VOYAGE OF COLUMBUS IN 1492
- Queen Isabella and King Ferdinand of Spain
- The Niña, Pinta, and Santa Maria
- Columbus's mistaken identification of "Indies" and "Indians"
- The idea of what was, for Europeans, a "New World"

B. THE PILGRIMS
- The Mayflower
- Plymouth Rock
- Thanksgiving Day celebration

C. JULY 4, "INDEPENDENCE DAY"
- The "birthday" of our nation
- Democracy (rule of the people): Americans wanted to rule themselves instead of being ruled by a faraway king.
- Some people were not free: slavery in early America

IV. Presidents, Past and Present

TEACHERS: Introduce children to famous presidents, and discuss with them such questions as: What is the president? How does a person become president? Who are some of our most famous presidents, and why?

See below, Symbols and Figures: Mount Rushmore; the White House.

- George Washington
    The "Father of His Country"
    Legend of George Washington and the cherry tree
- Thomas Jefferson, author of Declaration of Independence
- Abraham Lincoln
    Humble origins
    "Honest Abe"
- Theodore Roosevelt
- Current United States president

V. Symbols and Figures

- Recognize and become familiar with the significance of
    American flag
    Statue of Liberty
    Mount Rushmore
    The White House

Visual Arts: Kindergarten

SEE PAGE 3, "The Arts in the Curriculum."

TEACHERS: In schools, lessons on the visual arts should illustrate important elements of making and appreciating art, and emphasize important artists, works of art, and artistic concepts. When appropriate, topics in the visual arts may be linked to topics in other disciplines. While the following guidelines specify a variety of artworks in different media and from various cultures, they are not intended to be comprehensive. Teachers are encouraged to build upon the core content and expose children to a wide range of art and artists.

I. Elements of Art

TEACHERS: The generally recognized elements of art include line, shape, form, space, light, texture, and color. In kindergarten, introduce children to line and color. Engage students in recognizing and using different kinds of lines and colors, and point out lines and colors in nature. (You may also wish to observe shapes in art and nature—see Math: Geometry.)

A. COLOR
- Observe how colors can create different feelings and how certain colors can seem "warm" (red, orange, yellow) or "cool" (blue, green, purple)
- Observe the use of color in
  Pieter Bruegel, *The Hunters in the Snow*
  Helen Frankenthaler, *Blue Atmosphere*
  Paul Gauguin, *Tahitian Landscape*
  Pablo Picasso, *Le Gourmet*

B. LINE
- Identify and use different lines: straight, zigzag, curved, wavy, thick, thin
- Observe different kinds of lines in
  Katsushika Hokusai, *Tuning the Samisen*
  Henri Matisse, *The Purple Robe*
  Joan Miró, *People and Dog in the Sun*

II. Sculpture

- Recognize and discuss the following as sculptures:
  Northwest American Indian totem pole
  Statue of Liberty
- Mobiles: Alexander Calder's *Lobster Trap and Fish Tail*

See also American History K, Native Americans, *re* totem pole.

III. Looking at and Talking about Works of Art

TEACHERS: After children have been introduced to some elements of art and a range of artworks and artists, engage them in looking at pictures and talking about them. Ask the children about their first impressions—what they notice first, and what the picture makes them think of or feel. Go on to discuss the lines and colors, details not obvious at first, why they think the artist chose to depict things in a certain way, etc.

- Observe and talk about
  Pieter Bruegel, *Children's Games*
  Mary Cassatt, *The Bath*
  Winslow Homer, *Snap the Whip*
  Diego Rivera, *Mother's Helper*
  Henry O. Tanner, *The Banjo Lesson*

Music: Kindergarten

SEE PAGE 3, "The Arts in the Curriculum."

<u>TEACHERS:</u> In schools, lessons on music should feature activities and works that illustrate important musical concepts and terms, and should introduce important composers and works. When appropriate, topics in music may be linked to topics in other disciplines.

The following guidelines focus on content, not performance skills, though many concepts are best learned through active practice (singing, clapping rhythms, playing instruments, etc.).

I.   Elements of Music

- Through participation, become familiar with some basic elements of music (rhythm, melody, harmony, form, timbre, etc.).

    Recognize a steady beat; begin to play a steady beat.

    Recognize that some beats have accents (stress).

    Move responsively to music (marching, walking, hopping, swaying, etc.).

    Recognize short and long sounds.

    Discriminate between fast and slow.

    Discriminate between obvious differences in pitch: high and low.

    Discriminate between loud and quiet.

    Recognize that some phrases are the same, some different.

    Sing unaccompanied, accompanied, and in unison.

II.   Listening and Understanding

<u>TEACHERS:</u>   To encourage listening skills and the beginnings of understanding, play various kinds of music often and repeatedly. In the kindergarten classroom, music can be played for enjoyment, to accompany activities, to inspire creative movement, etc. Expose children to a wide range of music, including children's music, popular instrumental music, and music from various cultures.

<u>NOTE:</u> Grieg's "In the Hall of the Mountain King" is a good work to illustrate dynamics (loud and quiet), as well as tempo (slow and fast).

- Recognize the following instruments by sight and sound: guitar, piano, trumpet, flute, violin, drum.
- Become familiar with the following works:

    Edvard Grieg, "Morning" and "In the Hall of the Mountain King" from *Peer Gynt*

    Victor Herbert, "March of the Toys" from *Babes in Toyland*

    Richard Rodgers, "March of the Siamese Children" from *The King and I*

    Camille Saint-Saëns, *Carnival of the Animals*

III. Songs

<u>TEACHERS:</u> See also Language Arts, Mother Goose poems. A number of the poems may be sung to familiar melodies.

The Bear Went Over the Mountain

Bingo

The Farmer in the Dell

Go In and Out the Window

Go Tell Aunt Rhody

Here We Go Round the Mulberry Bush

The Hokey Pokey

Hush Little Baby

If You're Happy and You Know It
Jingle Bells
John Jacob Jingleheimer Schmidt
Kumbaya
London Bridge
Old MacDonald Had a Farm
Row, Row, Row Your Boat
This Old Man
Twinkle Twinkle Little Star
The Wheels on the Bus

TEACHERS: You may wish to supplement the songs listed above with songs from the Core Knowledge Preschool Sequence, as follows:

A Tisket, A Tasket
Are You Sleeping?
Blue-Tail Fly (Jimmie Crack Corn)
Do Your Ears Hang Low?
Did You Ever See a Lassie?
Eensy, Weensy Spider
Five Little Ducks That I Once Knew
Five Little Monkeys Jumping On the Bed
Happy Birthday to You
Head and Shoulders, Knees and Toes
Here is the Beehive
I Know an Old Lady
I'm a Little Teapot
Kookaburra
Lazy Mary
Looby Loo
Oats, Peas, Beans and Barley Grow
Oh, Do You Know the Muffin Man?
Oh Where, Oh Where, Has My Little Dog Gone?
One Potato, Two Potato
Open, Shut Them
Pop Goes the Weasel
Teddy Bear, Teddy Bear, Turn Around
Teddy Bears' Picnic
Where is Thumbkin?
Who Stole the Cookie from the Cookie Jar?
You Are My Sunshine

Mathematics: Kindergarten

TEACHERS: Mathematics has its own vocabulary and patterns of thinking. It is a discipline with its own language and conventions. Thus, while some lessons may offer occasional opportunities for linking mathematics to other disciplines, it is critically important to attend to math as math. From the earliest years, mathematics requires incremental review and steady practice: not only the diligent effort required to master basic facts and operations, but also thoughtful and varied practice that approaches problems from a variety of angles, and gives children a variety of opportunities to apply the same concept or operation in different types of situations. While it is important to work toward the development of "higher-order problem-solving skills," it is equally important—indeed, it is prerequisite to achieving "higher order" skills—to have a sound grasp of basic facts, and an automatic fluency with fundamental operations.

I. Patterns and Classification

- Establish concepts of likeness and difference by sorting and classifying objects according to various attributes: size, shape, color, amount, function, etc.
- Define a set by the common property of its elements.
- In a given set, indicate which item does not belong.
- Moving from concrete objects to pictorial representations, recognize patterns and predict the extension of a pattern.
- Extend a sequence of ordered concrete objects.

II. Numbers and Number Sense

- Using concrete objects and pictorial representations, compare sets:
  same as (equal to)
  more than
  less than
  most
  least
- Count
  forward from 1 to 31, first beginning with 1, and later from any given number
  backward from 10
  from 1 to 10 by twos
  by fives and tens to 50
- Recognize and write numbers 1 to 31 (with special attention to the difference between certain written symbols, such as: 6 and 9; 2 and 5; 1 and 7; 12 and 21, etc.).
- Count and write the number of objects in a set.
- Given a number, identify one more, one less.
- Identify ordinal position, first (1st) through sixth (6th).
- Identify pairs.
- Interpret simple pictorial graphs.
- Identify $\frac{1}{2}$ as one of two equal parts of a region or object; find $\frac{1}{2}$ of a set of concrete objects.

III. Money

- Identify pennies, nickels, dimes, and quarters.
- Identify the one-dollar bill.
- Identify the dollar sign ($) and cents sign (¢).
- Write money amounts using the cents sign (¢).

IV. Computation

- Add and subtract to ten, using concrete objects.
- Recognize the meaning of the plus sign (+).
- Subtraction: the concept of "taking away"; recognize the meaning of the minus sign (-).

V. Measurement

- Identify familiar instruments of measurement, such as ruler, scale, thermometer.
- Compare objects according to:
  Linear measure
  - long and short; longer than, shorter than
  - measure length using non-standard units
  - begin to measure length in inches
  - height: taller than, shorter than
  Weight (mass)
  - heavy, light
  - heavier than, lighter than
  Capacity (volume)
  - full and empty
  - less full than, as full as, fuller than
  Temperature: hotter and colder
- Time
  Sequence events: before and after; first, next, last.
  Compare duration of events: which takes more or less time.
  Read a clock face and tell time to the hour.
  Know the days of the week and the months of the year.
  Orientation in time: today, yesterday, tomorrow; morning, afternoon; this morning vs. yesterday morning, etc.

VI. Geometry

- Identify left and right hand.
- Identify top, bottom, middle.
- Know and use terms of orientation and relative position, such as:
  - closed, open
  - on, under, over
  - in front, in back (behind)
  - between, in the middle of
  - next to, beside
  - inside, outside
  - around
  - far from, near
  - above, below
  - to the right of, to the left of
  - here, there
- Identify and sort basic plane figures: square, rectangle, triangle, circle.
- Identify basic shapes in a variety of common objects and artifacts (windows, pictures, books, buildings, cars, etc.).
- Recognize shapes as the same or different.
- Make congruent shapes and designs.
- Compare size of basic plane figures (larger, smaller).

Science: Kindergarten

TEACHERS: Effective instruction in science requires hands-on experience and observation. In the words of the 1993 report from the American Association for the Advancement of Science, Benchmarks for Science Literacy, "From their very first day in school, students should be actively engaged in learning to view the world scientifically. That means encouraging them to ask questions about nature and to seek answers, collect things, count and measure things, make qualitative observations, organize collections and observations, discuss findings, etc."

While experience counts for much, book learning is also important, for it helps bring coherence and order to a child's scientific knowledge. Only when topics are presented systematically and clearly can children make steady and secure progress in their scientific learning. The child's development of scientific knowledge and understanding is in some ways a very disorderly and complex process, different for each child. But a systematic approach to the exploration of science, one that combines experience with book learning, can help provide essential building blocks for deeper understanding at a later time.

I. Plants and Plant Growth

TEACHERS: Through reading aloud, observation, and activities such as growing plants from seeds in varying conditions, explore the following with children:

- What plants need to grow: sufficient warmth, light, and water
- Basic parts of plants: seed, root, stem, branch, leaf
- Plants make their own food.
- Flowers and seeds: seeds as food for plants and animals (for example, rice, nuts, wheat, corn)
- Two kinds of plants: deciduous and evergreen
- Farming
    How some food comes from farms as crops
    How farmers must take special care to protect their crops from weeds and pests
    How crops are harvested, kept fresh, packaged, and transported for people to buy and consume

II. Animals and Their Needs

TEACHERS: Through reading aloud, observation, and activities, explore with children the common characteristics and needs of animals, including:

- Animals, like plants, need food, water, and space to live and grow.
- Plants make their own food, but animals get food from eating plants or other living things.
- Offspring are very much (but not exactly) like their parents.
- Most animal babies need to be fed and cared for by their parents; human babies are especially in need of care when young.
- Pets have special needs and must be cared for by their owners.

III. The Human Body

- The five senses and associated body parts:
    Sight: eyes
    Hearing: ears
    Smell: nose
    Taste: tongue
    Touch: skin
- Taking care of your body: exercise, cleanliness, healthy foods, rest

IV. Introduction to Magnetism

TEACHERS: Through reading aloud, observation, and experiments with magnets, introduce children to the idea that there are forces we cannot see that act upon objects. Children should:

- Identify familiar everyday uses of magnets (for example, in toys, in cabinet locks, in "refrigerator magnets," etc.).
- Classify materials according to whether they are or are not attracted by a magnet.

V. Seasons and Weather

TEACHERS: The emphasis in kindergarten should be on observation and description; technical explanations of meteorological phenomena should be taken up in later grades; see grades 2 and 4 for more detailed study of Meteorology.

- The four seasons
- Characteristic local weather patterns during the different seasons
- The sun: source of light and warmth
- Daily weather changes
    Temperature: thermometers are used to measure temperature
    Clouds
    Rainfall: how the condition of the ground varies with rainfall; rainbows
    Thunderstorms: lightning and thunder, hail, safety during thunderstorms
    Snow and snowflakes, blizzard

VI. Taking Care of the Earth

- Conservation: Some natural resources are limited, so people must be careful not to use too much of them (example: logging and reforestation).
- Practical measures for conserving energy and resources (for example, turning off unnecessary lights, tightly turning off faucets, etc.)
- Some materials can be recycled (for example, aluminum, glass, paper).
- Pollution (for example, littering, smog, water pollution) can be harmful, but if people are careful they can help reduce pollution.

VII. Science Biographies

George Washington Carver
Jane Goodall
Wilbur and Orville Wright

Notes

Notes

Notes

Core Knowledge Preschool At a Glance

	Knowledge and Skills

Movement and Coordination
I. Physical Attention and Relaxation
II. Gross Motor Skills
III. Eye-Hand and Eye-Foot Coordination
IV. Group Games
V. Creative Movement and Expression

Autonomy and Social Skills
I. Sense of Self and Personal Responsibility
II. Working in a Group Setting

Work Habits
I. Memory Skills
II. Following Directions
III. Task Persistence and Completion

Language
I. Oral Language
II. Nursery Rhymes, Poems, Fingerplays and Songs
III. Storybook Reading and Storytelling
IV. Emerging Literacy Skills

Mathematics
I. Patterns and Classification
II. Geometry
III. Measurement
IV. Numbers and Number Sense
V. Addition and Subtraction with Concrete Objects
VI. Money

Orientation in Time & Space
Time:
I. Vocabulary
II. Measures of Time
III. Passage of Time (Past, Present and Future)

Space:
I. Vocabulary
II. Actual and Represented Space
III. Simple Maps
IV. Basic Geographical Concepts

Science
I. Human Characteristics, Needs and Development
II. Animal Characteristics, Needs and Development
III. Plant Characteristics, Needs and Growth
IV. Physical Elements (Water, Air, Light)
V. Tools

Music
I. Attention to Differences in Sound
II. Imitate and Produce Sounds
III. Listen and Sing
IV. Listen and Move

Visual Arts
I. Attention to Visual Detail
II. Creating Art (Printing, Painting, Drawing, Collage, Sculpture)
III. Looking At and Talking About Art